AF346236

FUDGING LARUELLE'S DECISION

Magnus – Ingens – Immanis
mensurā (opp. parvus)

Grandis *incremento (a crescere ; opp. exilis, exiguus).*
Amplus/Vastus *spatio (opp. artus, angustus).*
Enormis *de quoquo extra normam vel mensuram
(opp. Modicus).*
Ingens *est immensus ; plus est quam* Magnus.
Immanis *est ingens, sed etiam aliquando timore et stupore
animos replet.*

Vastus *de loco* Amplo *et deserto dicitur.*

The collection of Immensity
Notebooks *is the pendant, in
volumes, of the revue* Condition
Zero. *Like this one, it is dedicated,
intimately and inexorably,
to* Immanence, *to* Theoria, *and to*
The Anthropos-Inmost.

Narciso Aksayam

FUDGING LARUELLE'S DECISION

A HISTORICAL PATH TOWARDS A NON-PHILOSOPHICAL BODY

IMMENSITY NOTEBOOKS

Immensity notebooks

A book series directed by
Narciso Aksayam
and
Gérard Comlan Kponsou

ISSN : 2780-6391
ISBN : 978-2-492346-06-4
Propriété intellectuelle, morale et *copyright*
Narciso Aksayam & INgens, 2023
4, rue des Cloyères
10380 Plancy-L'Abbaye
FRANCE

*Phenomenology is not
an element but a resonance,
a chain or an economy of
effects from which we
draw, precisely in order to
give to some of its effects the
authenticity of their concept.*

Fr. Laruelle

THE ECONOMY OF EFFECTS-OF-BEING

(1974) vol. 1, p. 37.

*For Jesse Newberg and Jeremy Ross Smith,
with the deepest respect.*

Foreword

History's getting fast.

Actually only when details are going missing, sinking into oblivion or fading among dispersive heaps, sealed by erosions.

History is like Borges' Funès – or better : like Mr. Albert, as Marc-Antoine Mathieu's *Mutation* told the story – : when memory lacks matter, the story that is told gets shorter.

But getting shorter makes History more handy to roam, more schematic to overview and more essential to embrace. That is precisely what is at stake for the economy of the ones who don't want to live in the past, stuck in sediments, mesmerized in drowning details, but who are eager not to get lost out of the streams of the civilization they emerge from, as praxes and as vivid meanings, in continuous lines of invention passing through the universe they fuel.

Part of the present text consists in a comprehensive scheme for a historical compound. In fact, it is somehow a spread of references, a volley of dates and contexts, a squirt of coordinates that operates like a shortcut, like an instant lightning, for the reader to penetrate the very spillage of duration and events out of which something like generations organize their understanding of experience – here precisely, of that specific experience we clepe *Body*.

Yet there is no such thing as a shortcut in Thought. One cannot lean on anybody to make the work of reading, of meditating, of understanding, and to set the exploration of one's own and oneself requisite by Thought as such : there is no impersonation in thinking, neither in exploring nor in experiencing. Especially when encountering the apparatus of thoughts that has been moulded by somebody else ; impersonation is precisely the manner to avoid encountering or being encountered. Unless, might be the case, if you strive for a parrot career in Thought – which can be, let's acknowledge it, at the very least colourful…

Cultural sprouts and blossoms leave as many seeds, as many semens – as many *pollens*, like Novalis says – as you can count on a list of names, of titles, of theorems, dropped by incidents, by collisions, by interrupted storylines of depleted lives, or by ephemeral synopses built out of transient knowledge. The present text is meant to shape a gutter, a trough to gather the elusive structure of one of these name-droppings that constitutes a significant path towards both conceptions of embodiment and stakes of contemporary cutting-edge thoughts.

But in no way the mapping will spare you the hike.

Il n'y a plus de philosophie
si l'on regarde d'abord aux conclusions ;
le philosophe ne cherche pas les raccourcis,
il fait toute la route.

Maurice Merleau-Ponty[1]

* * *

Contemporary Philosophy has both collided and collapsed from Rationalism (*i.e.* post-Renaissance modernist expectancies and

---

[1] « There is no more Philosophy if you jump to conclusions first ; the philosopher doesn't look for shortcuts, he goes all the road. », in *Bergson se faisant* [Bergson shaping himself], 1959.

plans) into Nihilism ; from the normative logical discovery and mastery (or scheduling) of Nature into the inner experience of radical freedom (*i.e.* lived emptiness and loneliness) in constituting meaning and individual architectured significance[2].

Philosophy having become an extensive cultural equipment, at first for Europeans but tendentially world-wide, any current subject — may it be a race activist moving ahead ideological pawns, a TV show-addict prowling for the next daily shot of streaming, a

---

[2] Such a statement is at least true for philosophies that have concerns with long-lasting storylines (with the Becoming of civilizations, with the anthropological transformation of Meaning, or with the current state of universality projects, for example a unified and consistent scientific modelization of reality based on institutionalized common references for measures and for logical operations).

But for philosophies that have concerns with the quality of statements, and with the kind of operations for which statements are a field of application, rather than concerns with the continuation or the continuity of stories, myths or empirical History, such a statement rises very few interests, and carries, if it does in any sense, some very weak truth.

Just to be clear .

(Though at least both epistemological, anthropological and gnoseological matters are at stake here for any kind of philosophy to ground its decisions and its expectancies...)

dedicated and/or neurotic transgendered housewife watering permacultural plantations, or a frenzied NFT trader bargaining one's multimedia influence… – is every day concerned by the using of these tools and cultural accessories, and currently experiences, as a being shaped, defined and kneaded by it, this epochal *situation* (and this last word is precisely chosen for its resonances with the Existentialist conceptual narrative, at the very least from Jean-Paul Sartre to Guy Debord).

Yet, only intent and purposeful theorists possess the levers and the analytic sights on the articulations of this whole cultural endorsement, which permeates our impulses of understanding and which irrigates the lives of deeds that stem from. Probably the only asset that brings professionalism in Philosophy.

For the mainstream jays of Philosophy, whom we daily have to get along with, the current *paradigm* that frames our existential experience has something to do with something alike or related to the kickshaw of *Deconstruction*. Delicacy of high-graduated and high-educated people, to indulge in dismantling the symbolic, the codes and order that most struggle a whole youth, even some a whole life, to get to.

As if *construction* wasn't a psychiatric jeopardy, in which the comfortable well-off of mental health can play cultural games that are at risk for the less endowed, if not at their expense...

But let's take the issue the other way round :

Only people who haven't ever read one page of Derrida can be offended by the comparison of Deconstruction with a delicate and dandy *unsubstantial* dish — at least from an Aristotelian point of view. But if everyone talking about Deconstruction had ever read some Derrida, we would be living in a time of ontologists.

We are not.

So let's put it this way :

If you consider psychological constructions as distortions or even as deformities, or if you take cultural and educational inheritance as bias or prejudice on the bases of which lies misunderstanding, injustice, disfigurement of reality, or even the deepest way of exaction or of extortion of one's self ; and if you assume that there is underneath, below the sedimentation of these influences and below these deceptive lessons of order, a true experience that has to be saved, restored, or reached in whatever the way –, then you can just consider constructions as mere obstacles to be bypassed, to be overcome or to be overturned.

And Deconstruction is then not only legitimate, but it is THE way, the only way, to knowledge, to freedom, to justice, and to real encounter – with oneself, with others, and above all with the Real.

Ontologically speaking, what we call Deconstruction takes place in the movement of an Immanence theoretical quest :

How to access undubitable Truth from a subjective point of view on my immediate cognitive activity (Descartes) *?*

How to assess and evaluate Reason with no tools of judgment taken out of Reason itself, and how to explore the limits of Reason from within the Reason itself (Kant) *?*

How to embrace the tragedy of life and endorse it from the deepest and most intense sentiment of approval, without trying to redeem pain and disappointment with the promises of another world, worthier than the actual terrestrial one (Nietzsche) *?*

[but we can go back further in time :
How to exert human existence under a realm of sole human laws (Humanism) *? How to follow a*

sacred call from the inner experience of one's own conscience (Augustin) And even : *How to experience Deity from the mortal point of view of flesh — and reversibly, how to experience humanhood from a miraculous divine ascendency* (Jesus Christ) ? etc.]

When founding Phenomenology at the beginning of the xx[th] century, Edmund Husserl ultimately radicalized this demand, this theoretical yearning for immanence, by asking :

How to scientifically ground and assert both any individual lived, any single subjective experience, and the eidetic continuity of identity that gathers the stream of sketches that temporo-spatial perception provides to us ?

And answering such a question, by giving an experimental tool, able to turn any knowledge back into the *lived intuition* where it was rooted, able to bring any consciousness back to its indivision with the very phenomenon it primitively coincides with :

Ἐποχή, *i.e.* the phenomenological Reduction.

Being able to put any acquired knowledge into brackets, — may it be all at once with full agency on the operation, like Husserl described his process, or may it be a progressive transition, gaining one silent step after the other, for days, like a disease we contract inadvertently, in the way Sartre describes his *Nausea* –, that's the precise apparatus where Deconstruction finds its intimate possibility[3].

However, it is Heidegger who introduced *stricto sensu* the topic of unbuilding the metaphysical sediments of meaning (*Abbau*). By doing so, he was drawing all the consequences of the input of Interpretation, instead of the univocal logical normativity assumed by Husserl's late rationalism, as the major philosophical process of constituting meaning – *i.e.* an artistic process, setting free the metaphorical might of Philosophy, and registering Nietzsche's ontological claims that meaning consists in a cruel, agonistic and relentless theatre of conflict between the denying and compensatory delusion of weak gregarious forces, and the inventive and empowering saltatory dance in intensity of rare individualistic aristocratic wills of potency.

That is what made Phenomenology coincide with Postmodernism. And that is the legacy Derrida has gotten from Heidegger and has passed on to us : an aristocratic manner to deal with native uncertainty of meaning – in

---

[3] Further details on this in Narciso Aksayam, *Sartre, la Réduction jusqu'à la lie* [Sartre : Reduction, gulped until dregs] (FR-Plancy-L'Abbaye : Ingens, 2021).

other words : a dandystic way to reside within an unsubstantial real, within the realm of sovereign Nihilism.

We have to make here two things clear.

This Heidegger phenomenological assumption of Postmodernism (Nietzsche's) was a way of introducing Husserl's protocol of immanence into Finitude, *i.e.* to draw the Absolute into contingency. But it was also an attempt to drive the scientific *transcendental ego*, the abstract subject of knowledge, into an existential *ethos*, as a *Dasein* [a human open space of experience, *i.e.* a situated/situating existence] immerged inside penetrating climates of Being, fatally prompted by raw angst into act, that is, into politics, or at least into being concerned with the turnings of civilization, that is, *collective meaning of existence.*

Heideggerian finitude and Fate (Destiny) appear by striking Husserl's methodology at its core : the phenomenological Reduction. For Heidegger, ἐποχή is not a deliberate operation processed by a free imagination and an act of judgment of the phenomenologist anymore ; ἐποχή is envisioned from that moment onwards as an infra-rational event, a shift inside mood, which provides its ontological effects under the guise of boredom, or of anguish, of æsthetic sentiment, if not of daring hazard or near-death experiences... which are all experiences of nothingness swooping down on being – experiences of nihil deeply penetrating and working life at its edge[4].

What this turn introduced into Phenomenology was *passivity* (*i.e.* a loss of agency for the subject of experience, and the complete operation of Phenomenology tending to be experienced in the form of a call, questioning from Being, rather than a scientific research initiative, and above all rather than an operation pertaining to the enframing of a *Tékhnè*), passivity and *intersubjectivity* (*i.e.* an essential permeability, patency, to infra-rational – even *pre-noetic* – collective experiences of meaning : cultural ambiance, meaning climates).

This question of Finitude is crucial.

[4] Husserl explicitly reproached Heidegger for having brought back from the World War I front a mysticism of Death, which seemingly withdrew into an Eckart-like negative theology that Husserl acknowledges to feel close to, and from which this mysticism of Death flew back onto ontology. See Dorion Cairns, *Conversations with Husserl and Fink* (The Hague : Nijhoff, 1976).

Especially in the case of immanence. It is the question of experiencing borders and limitations, but from the inside. It even eventually becomes the philosophical attempt to explain – or to embrace a comprehension of – the very being of limitation itself, without referring or resorting to any kind of « exteriority ».

And finitude has many avatars.

For Heidegger, among other variations, Time shapes an intimate Finitude and an intimate relation to Finitude, under the guise of Being-towards-Death and under the existential syntaxis of ecstasy (*i.e.* over-boarding, standing beyond standing, exceeding).

But another kind of Finitude can be overcome by the means of the dread that comes with the former one : the Pascalian finitude of amusements, which is a guise of the Senecian diversions, can be converted into Authenticity (*Eigentlichkeit*) through the experience of angst that comes as the Heideggerian phenomenological reduction ; the absorption of the *Dasein*/existential subject in the unauthentical « They » (in a meaningless life) can be redeemed, in such a way that the finitude (of the limited existential consciousness) is transubstantiated by embracing another finitude, a more essential/immanent one… The horizon of Death opens the *Dasein* to its utmost possibility and reveals to itself its inmost identity – which are its most appropriate appearance as well as its most fatal/destined presence to itself (*Ereignis*), that has been lost, locked or refrained under the gregarious unauthenticity of the « They ».

Derrida is somehow in the direct continuity of Heidegger, although now focused on linguistics' cares, when he writes :

> « The relationship with *my death* (my disappearance in general) thus lurks in this determination of being as presence, ideality, the absolute possibility of repetition. The possibility of the sign is this relationship with death. »[5]

This may help to understand the specific relation Derrida ontologically sets with Finitude. Derrida operates a theoretical substitution between Husserl's transcendental consciousness (or Heidegger's sentimental *Dasein*) and a pantextualist conception of experience.

[5] Jacques Derrida, *Speech and Phenomena*, chap. IV « Meaning and representation » (Evanston : Northwestern University Press, 1973)

If Death and disappearance are the very possibilities for the linguistic sign, the consciousness – as capable of meanings, of expressions, of remembrances as well of projections (futuritions) – is from that moment onwards (but actually from always already ever) counted as a full textual field, that is, a field constituted with nothing but traces, nothing but signs indicating towards something absent, already gone or not yet to come.

The whole conscious horizon of experience is henceforth only woven with unpresent, differed, tendentially erased elements, towards which Being is "essentially" (but not properly) oriented.

In such a theoretical set, the phenomenon being structurally a textual experience, the phenomenological Reduction consists – not in putting knowledge and judgments into brackets (Husserl style), not in dipping utensil understandings of the World into atmospheres, climates, of nothingness (Heidegger style) – but in putting portions (shares) of text into quotation marks.

If there is immanently nothing outside textual-like structures to be experienced, then everything is absent within the presence of its very indication ; then every being refers to something else by being essentially missing where it appears as such ; then every element of experience can be quoted as being imputed, *ascribed* to someone else, to something else, to some other thing.

And Reduction consists then in an inner experience of the text/in the text, that compels to Alterity, that drives to the utmost/inmost otherness where the *ego* usually, traditionally, abides.

Although there is no authenticity to be reached in such an apparatus anymore, or even to be aimed at, like it was the ambition in Heidegger's conception, Derrida, as the son and heir of *Abbau* and Postmodernism, shares with Heidegger a decisive plot, both an effect and a praxis of their philosophical orientations : the uncertain non-normative neither univocal use of language, may it be Speech or may it be Text, on which relies an essentially hermeneutical regard towards meaning, *i.e.* a finite practice of language as a utensil, the ending of language as a docile, submissive *Tekhnè* of meaning.

And by saying *decisive*, something means to be carefully handled, cautiously heard, attentively listened to :

Passing from Heidegger's philosophy to Derrida's, there is no mystery that this effective finitude affecting our meanings and our power of understanding is transferred from a para-fascist ethnocentric sentimentalism to a liberal cosmopolitan avant-garde textualism ; *i.e.* from a former Catholic adulator of the German National Socialism to a native French-Algerian Jewish atheist.

Here is the second thing to be cleared.

At an individual level, both Heidegger and Derrida evolve under a historical Nietzschean influence. They wield philosophy as being an art practice, for which meaning is a raw material to be explored, to be kneaded, to be sculpted, may it be by Poetry or by the search of an authentic *etymon*, or may it be by a textual variation around unfathomable repetitions or by the asymptotic exploration of the ambivalent meaning of meaning.

By bringing thus to its climax the potency of interpretation, both remain under the spectrum of an artistic metaphysics, which confronts the unlinear intents of invention with the unpredictable aspects of a changing matter, the will at its utmost sovereignty and insubmission with the challenge of encountering sensibility, one's own but also the other's, at the limits of collectiveness – which are, by definition, reversible with the limits of the individual.

At this level of existential collective meaningfulness, unprecedented creative freedom, incandescent sovereignty, radical resharpening of significations, are then not only a point of anthropology, the point of confronting human with the intangible openness of giving sense ; but it is also (first and foremost, are we sure ?) a point of politics, the point of dealing with instability of significance, the query affecting hierarchies, identities and essences, borders and limits having to be *decided* from the field of an ungrounded truth, *i.e.* from the most complete acknowledged state of Nihilism.

What is to be emphasized, politically speaking or anthropologically speaking, is that Nihilism is what Far-Right and Judaism share : the uncertainty of meaning, either from a Decline or from an essential alterity of the origins of Meaning.

But they adopt a different attitude regarding how the might faces the impotency : Far-Right claims that there is a Golden Age to be reconquered back to its former state of mastery or of glory (and this *reconquesta* is most of the time described as a decolonization war, willing for a restoration of sovereignty against decadent or invasive insiders, willing for the restoration of the highest Authenticity against the denial contamination of the « They ») ; Judaism acknowledges Nihilism to be the form of an ordinary finitude of the human condition, and to open an infinite field for an infinite work, not to be achieved but to be every time anew resumed and revived from the beginning, from an infinitely untraceable beginning…

How to proceed from Nihilism, from originary anarchy, from structural a-significance, from an essential innominability or from an abyssal chaos of encroachment among ambivalent meanings ? : this was the philological question injected by Nietzsche into the philosophical organism. Heidegger and Derrida form a dyad of metabolization of this semantic insemination into European culture, a dyad at the same time opposite and homogeneous, at the same time diametric and homologous. They both adopt the philological interpretative or hermeneutic attitude, both swallowing, both withstanding, the announcement of the event of the death of God. And they both confront the reversibility of finitude and opening, of ambition and humility, of dread and invigoration that characterizes Nihilism.

But from a Judaic perspective, Derrida carries out an endorsement of the limits of agency, within the very structure of consciousness (as being a text) – and by doing so, he embraces somehow the Nietzschean *amor fati* ; while Heidegger awaits and/or announces (prophesies ?), from a para-pagan messianic perspective, the restoration of agency to its supreme idealized form, both under the guise of a new sacred, on the verge of its manifestation, and under the guise of the late rediscovery of a golden age of the understanding of Being : the pre-Socratic age – and by doing so, he embraces somehow the structural promise of the forthcoming *Übermensch*…

Precisely, one of the most incumbent questions that comes with Nihilism is to sieve, between its many effects, the fascist effects and the emancipating ones (or revolutionary ones) – knowing that they are both of the ambiguous kind of the empowering effects (that have first to be sorted from the Nihilism's despairing, devoiding, downcasting effects)…

How to *decide* which are which, which can be isolated from which, which are correlated with which, which have selective effects on which, or which are intimately contaminated by, intrinsically impregnated with, even essentially mixed with and mixtes of, or are unsuspected masks of which ?

* * *

The present essay is, in its own manner, an extension, a pseudopod of these questions, of this *kind* of questions, once you have abstracted them into manifesting their structural syntaxis of operation.

It is a tentacle of contemporary thoughts – in the way they refine their processes and draw all the consequences of their machinery –, groping, fumbling inside, to raise new reliefs in the matter (of) thought ; but it takes also contemporary thoughts as objects to be analysed, to be set for experiment, following the protocol of Laruelle's Non-Philosophy, a protocol which precisely grew within the cradle of Heidegger's and/or Derrida's Deconstruction, within the spectre of these Greek/Jewish questions, especially the question of *decision*[6].

---

[6] These questions are the questions of the Greek pagan continuous determinations for the share of power, confronted with the questions of the Jewish reception of the miraculous discontinuities from an

One can say, to sum it up as condensely as might be, that before he reached a theory of the *Philosophical Decision*, François Laruelle takled first for a long time with the touchy and tricky issues of parting revolutionary and potentizing effects from fascist and domineering effects inside the Nietzschean syntaxis of thought.

The difficulty was of the intrication and of the reversibility of these effects, except for one *irreducible* but non-thetic element, which always eludes Power and Domination, the object (r) ; an object that assumed many names in Laruelle's outlinings, until it took one of the most rebellious, maybe insurrectionary names, the name of the inmost inherent lived that eludes the utmost authority, that of Philosophy itself, and this name was : the *One*.

To say it shortly, an immanent residue had to make a *differance*, by being both an element

unreachable and unshareable unique power.
Maïmonides has set these questions side by side ; Laruelle, as coming from a Christian Protestant culture, made the attempt to diagnose and to dose the possible mixtures of Greek and Jewish that have been inherited by Modern Philosophy through the remains of the Roman Christianization of Europe, *i.e.* to sort what pertains to knowledge, to free will,, to significancy, to passivity, to transcendence, to human agency.

pertaining to (or intimately needed by) the operations of nihilism and at the same time a point of undomitable sovereignty escaping the syntaxis of effects of these operations. An uncatchable outer point, a non-thetic inner element, irreversibly in and out at the same time, depending on the transcendental point of view that is adopted by the theory ; a point which cannot be *decided*, but neither can be *deciding*, only *decisive* in the last instance, even fateful, at least for Philosophy itself.

To understand that point, we have to recall that *Decisionism* is what politically characterizes Fascism. The art of decision describes what Fascism opposes to parliamentary governances, as an art of rupture, an art of sovereign will, the art that converts the reflexive endless democratic discussion into an undebatable aristocratic deed.

And if art is conceptually evoked here, that is precisely because fascist individuality participates to artistic metaphysics. Fascism figures a political climax of the modern emancipation of the individual power, somewhere in-between imperialist romanticism and lonely political self-determination, mixing geniality, inebriating risk taking and immediate jouissance and usufruct of civilization changings impulsed from an uninfluencible consciousness, that is, a unilateral one.

Such a depiction of Fascism explains why it is so difficult to come to any conclusion when arguing about Heidegger's thought belonging or not to Nazism. For, although explicitly declinist, as pointed, and moreover ontologically (rather than racially) antisemitic, Heidegger's opposition to *Tekhnè* exhibits a deep contradiction with any objective, even methodological, exertion of power. Actually confronting our inner finitude, as Heideggerian Being calls us upon, carries us to embrace what Laruelle calls, in a Lévinassian reference which he increased with a textual mark of uncertainty : « un?power ».

When Laruelle launched his chase against/towards the Philosophical Decision, we have to understand that this was the continuation of his struggle against Fascism within the postmodern processes of thought, but enhanced through the generalisation of Deconstruction to the whole philosophical domain, from a scientific rather than a literary point of view, *i.e.* under an analytic or para-axiomatic process rather than a poetic and purely interpretative one – under a renewed normativity, but different from the Husserlian one, different from the rationalist one : a passive indifferent one, an un?powerful one, *i.e* a mystical One.

Laruelle's operation was both to neutralize the decision and to identify its complete syntaxis within the philosophical apparatus. But not only in the perspective of condemning it as an ultimate fascist afterglow inside Philosophy.

His program was to eventually set the philosophical decision free, free for being invented like it never had been before, through an irreversible act of democratization which lavishes – which hands out – unilaterality for every one, rather than letting it be mono- polized by some changing kinds of transient authority, may it be the ultimate form of authority ever on Thought and on Humanity : the philosophical one.

Doing so, Laruelle's heretical gesture consisted in both capturing the last fascist residues involved in philosophical processes and syntaxes (*i.e* structures), and in opening a new democratic field of avant-garde specu- lative experimentation, which coincides, as a result as well as its apriorical possibility, with an unprecedented emancipation of masses, the massification, at an anthropological level, of individual Christianity

In Laruelle's claim, Philosophy is characterized in the last instance by unelucidated, unspoken, denied, decisions that culminate within contemporary thought and its infinite variations (repetitions) of reversibility – especially the reversiblities that allow the ontologies relying on Difference (Nietzsche, Heidegger, Deleuze, Derrida, Lyotard…), *i.e.* the most comprehensive synthetic/analytic line of ontological delimitation for manifestation. The frenzied *circulus viciosus* of reversibility cannot be stopped *unless some radical Absolute is set*, an Absolute that *irreversibly cuts within reversibility*.

Inside Phenomenology, Emmanuel Lévinas exhibits the very first insights of this theoretical situation – which is a situation rather than an apparatus because it draws its radical structure from a trauma, *i.e.* an existential lived experience of irreversible cut.

Lévinas's theoretical matrix, that relies on Ethics rather than ontology (beyond it), apprehends this Absolute, both/neither resisting and/nor escaping the rational enframing of the concept (*i.e.* the *Technè* of Philosophy as such), as an absolute Alterity, that is, an unassumable and irreducible exteriority.

But exteriority is precisely what Philosophy has, each time ever, to decide ; exteriority is precisely what Philosophy cannot infer by its sole conceptual continuities, by the sole tools of its rational will, by its sole *Tekhnè*.

As soon as there is Alterity, as soon as there is exteriority, whatever coordinates Philosophy gives to it in its conceptual matrices, these coordinates have to be decided, in order for this experience of alterity to be clasped, handled, adjudicated. This is peculiarly the case in the contexts of contemporary interpretative reversibilities, for instance reversibilities that deal with what is whether outside or inside...

Laruelle's ordinary people consists in an answer to this kind of question : *Does what is exterior of Philosophy stands necessarily outside of humanity ?*

What happens, what kind of speculation results, from the decision to consider people living, experiencing somewhere else than within the realm of Philosophy ? What result from the decision to consider Philosophy and its productions, its effects and its causalities, as being extraneous to human essence ? What does the axiomatic hypothesis of some immediate *datum* being exterior to Philosophy, being radically beyond its reach, but at the same time – and for the first time – indivisibly interior, immanent (to) human essence... bring ou ?

Regarding the act of decision, Laruelle accuses philosophers, and perhaps Philosophy itself, to be in denial. As if philosophers didn't want to take account, to acknowledge, the fascist moment involved in their process. As if, more deeply, Philosophy didn't want decision to be emancipated, experienced and experimented, out of the range of use that the blind spot of denial allows inside rationality.

This being said in psychoanalytic terms.

But in Marxist terms, one could suggest that decision is this human force of labour which Philosophy palms, monopolizes and capitalizes for its own benefit and for the sole profit of its overgrowing authority over minorities... That is, Marxistly speaking, minorities are the ontological equivalent of what proletarians are on the basis of class sociology.

Inside Derrida's framework, one can now guess : this is decisions that are to be deconstructed ; this is decisions that have been sedimented, perverted and disguised under layers and layers of traces, culminating in a generalized ontological indecidability.

Inside Heidegger's framework, setting free decisions is setting free the guises of Being ; and destroying, unbuilding Metaphysics is struggling against the domination of one single effect of Being over the others, it is opening the operation of Being – which is an operation of meaning, of understanding – to the comprehension of its essence as a becoming (*Wesen*).

But how to decide whether Deconstruction is an emancipation or a destructing *circulus viciosus* ? How to decide if inherited laws, transmitted habits, educative injunctions or traditional Lore, are bequeathed treasures from the past lineage of generations, or a cancer of dominations suffocating individual psyches ? How to decide about a decision if it is a benediction or the very semen of Evil, the intimate germ of radical woe ?

* * *

If we get back where we started, History, especially History of Philosophy, can be apprehended in the last instance, from the point of experience of minorities, as a series of decisions :

Epistemological decisions between descriptions and prescription ; ontological decisions between Being and Becoming ; anthropological decisions between the noble savage and *Homo homini lupus* ; which led to political decisions between sacred laws and corrupting civilization ; that is, to theological decisions between the original sin and a golden age native virginity... all decisions that mostly result, according to Laruelle, in the monopolization of decidefullness under one sole authorithy (*Authority* being *per se* the name of the power to decide).

Laruelle himself, as he emerged and evolved from lines of Thought – lines within which one can follow the potencies of Kant, Fichte, Ravaisson, Nietzsche, Heidegger, Deleuze, Henry, even Simondon or Hottois... –, that is, as one can follow the genetics of his doctrine, the history and turning steps of the formation of his Non-Standard Thought (from a libidinal kind of deconstruction towards a musicological kind of mystics, *via* a non-philosophical heresy), – Laruelle himself genuinely operates several decisions which are focused on and brought to the forefront of his analyses and considerations, as being at the core of the philosophical phenomenon he confronts. One of the most important being the decision on which rely the root definitions of Transcendence, of Immanence, of Mixtures and above all the definition of Cut, *i.e.* of the peculiar henological subjectivity (but without neither *sub* nor *ject*, pure *ity*, pure identity without attributes).

Postulates, axioms, principles even proposals, and, above all, definitions are decisions. But each distributed with different kinds of authorities inside the syntaxes of Thought.

Actually Laruelle's program consists in pulverizing authority and in distributing it to minorities, in a free, inventive and unprecedented dispersive way. It consists, by the means of Deconstruction, to set free an infinite democracy of constructions, and to open inside Philosophy infinite possibilities of decisions, in order to set an infinite variation of unprecedented agreements, an infinite experimental setting of meanings by the means of the inmost outrageous abysmal meaningless experience, unbound Nihilism, one might say, Ray Brassier-style.

Yet, as being a syntax formalizer, Laruelle appears very modest, very discreet, if not hermetically silent, with names, empirical references, even with quotations, and more broadly with tracing or sourcing the historical determinations of his thought.

This methodological and stylistic decision can be traced very deep, very upstream, within his work. We can observe it from the very spring of his writings, at the opening of his PhD dissertation, when he warns :

> « Barely no quotations nor references will be found inside these researches. They were however produced by the systematic de-markage [differentiating] of/from three prime authors : Husserl, Heidegger, Deleuze, and of/from few others (Lévinas, Derrida, Klossowski) who aren't much more acknowledged. They yet do not pretend to any historical originality. They consist first in intellectual exercises that aim for academical ambitions. Produced in the margins of these three works, there is none of their words, none of their formulas, none of their movements of thought, that doesn't refer to them. The debt was too huge and too indivisible to be retailed at page footers. So one shall, please, not see in this silence an attempt to appropriate their thoughts which admittedly don't belong to me, neither in their diversity nor even, in a certain extent, as a whole. »[7]

Such an attitude can be interpreted as a reluctance to any kind of story-telling inside

[7] François Laruelle, *Économie des effets d'être, op. cit.*, vol. 1, « Warning » (Paris : Université de Nanterre, 1974).

the deploying of theory – even though the story might be of the etymological kind, telling the evolution of specific terms, like Heidegger introduced, in his way of telling the history of metaphysics ; or even though the story might proceed like a theatrical drama, the way Deleuze stressed in his analyses of *conceptual characters*.

It can also be interpreted as a reluctance to source experience as coming from a text, a reluctance to prolong thought as being the continuity of an endless (and origineless) *commentarium*, that is, the insight that the Ἐποχή could not be summarized to the mere practice of putting into quotation marks the discourse of the Other.

But this attitude attests an even more radical hostility towards the History of Philosophy, the deepest and most violent Laruellian reluctance against the contemporary tendency to turn the teaching of Philosophy into a mere narrative about former thinkers and ancient discourses and to turn philosophers, thinkers, into historians, a theoretical rigorous demand that culminated, in the early 80's, in the publication of « The Crimes of the History of Philosophy », a squib that Laruelle self-edited in his series of Notebooks *Why Not*

Philosophy ?[8], precisely at the time he was formulating his theory of the philosophical decision[9].

Still this decision in Laruelle's writing to act outside of the common posture of archæology within the traditional library-philosophy involves the disappearing of some coordinates of the genesis of his thought, the coordinates that names provide, as known-too-well-known previous works. And these coordinates manifest, by connecting statements with previous works, other kinds of philosophical decisions that have been then put into silence.

There are names that Laruelle has massively mobilised. We know them for being the names of the Philosophers of the Difference : Nietzsche, Heidegger, Deleuze, Derrida. There are names that Laruelle has confronted directly (Ravaisson, Fichte, Marx,…), repeatedly (Descartes, Kant, Lévinas,…) or punctually (Arendt, Eckhart, Henry,…) ; even names he

[8] François Laruelle. « Les Crimes de l'Histoire de la philosophie », in *Pourquoi pas la philosophie ?*, n°2, 1983 – reprinted in Narciso Aksayam (Ed.), #*TRANSISTOR* [DVD-ROM] (FR. Plancy-l'Abbaye : INgens, 2012).

[9] He was at that moment program director at the *Collège International de Philosophie*. See François Laruelle. « Théorie de la décision philosophique », in *Pourquoi pas la philosophie ?*, n°3, 1984 – reprinted in Narciso Aksayam (Ed.), #*TRANSISTOR* [DVD-ROM] (FR. Plancy-l'Abbaye : INgens, 2012).

pointed to only once (Serge Valdinoci), or referred to under cover (*Saint Gilles with a sword* a.k.a. Gilles Grelet). But one of the names that are surprisingly « absent » of his analyses is Sartre.

Why surprisingly ?

It is of course surprising within a horizon of expectancies…

Except for the « Warning » quoted above, metadiscourses on his own personal praxis are not that many in Laruelle's writings, especially about peculiar details – and even while presenting his praxis of experimental hyper-speculative texts, the ones which he soon called « Philofictions ». « There is no meta-language for saying what non-philosophy is or is capable of doing… », as he says in *Struggle and Utopia in the End Times of Philosophy*. There is none, unless, of course, you consider Non-Philosophy as being a main ferocious meta-discourse on/in Philosophy, and Laruelle as being himself THE Philosopher, the one whom he is experiencing about, the one whom he is living about, at an autobiographic trans-cendental level.

Looking into details, one of the key-praxes of Laruelle's discourse is his use of brakets over prepositions. *Same (of) the Difference* ; *Real (of) the One* ; *subjects (of) the science* ; *inherent (to) self* ; *immanence (of) the One* ; *given (to) itself without alienation* ; *we accede (to) the One, (to) Exteriority, (to) the Universe without language…* you name it.

This praxis manifests a unilateral duality/identity of (« (of) ») genitive use (thetic propriety) and appositive use (lived identity) – what Serge Valdinoci analyses as a *univers comma*, at the same time *of* and *in* ; but Valdinoci doesn't use brackets in his writings to operate this « uniduality », though he takes a deep account of this absolute syntaxis…

Yet when looking backwards into French xx[th] Century Philosophy, we can find a previous use of similar brackets, in Jean-Paul Sartre's *L'Être et le Néant*.

Of course, there is no point in having expected that Laruelle commented more than he did about this. Most of his analyses regarding Sartre are related to how the unreflexive non-thetic consciousness (of) self remains synthetic and withdrawn from Idealism, and to how the One must not be confused with Nothingness as it prevails in Phenomenology. But even in seeming opposition or differentiation, what catches our interest is that Laruelle shares with Sartre a lineage of *decision*, and precisely a lineage that has concerns with Anthropology, *i.e.* the essence of human.

Laruelle's ordinary human, the human-in-person, can be described as not reachable by descriptions, because not reachable by *logos*. The One has no attributes. The One-in-One is reluctant (by indifference) to any attempt of characterization by any of the tools of Philosophy, indifferently repulsive by unilaterally determining Being in the last instance. To tell it otherwise, the One, as being pure cut (without having been cut), is pure decision (without having been decided). It is what Philosophy feels free from Philosophy, a pure dispersive minority that is free from authority, without the necessity of being set free from authority, without the necessity of being liberated from it, by the means of a soon becoming new authority. The One (is) without from, given-without-giveness.

Sartre's pure freedom presents the same emptiness of determination in the situation of engagement.

As Raymond Ruyer, the incredible democrat of values and the early true eidetician of Multiple, pointed repeatedly, Existentialism, regarding freedom, is an exact continuation of the Kantian abstract liberty ; the existentialist freedom knows no relation to neither the finitude or determinations of the agent nor to the finitude or determinations of the context (otherwise you're exposed to being a « bastard ») ; and it has (prequelly or sequelly) no relation to anykind of teleological essences when drawing the aim of one's deed (otherwise essence would precede existence)[10].

When knowing that Ruyer has written a *Princeton Gnosis*, things begin to become sharply interesting, especially because Hans Jonas, the well-known specialist of Gnosticism, produced a ruthless attack against Sartre for being a gnosticist and an impenitent dualist[11].

We know that the influence of Ruyer on Deleuze is huge. The *plane of immanence*, the *escaping lines…* are conceptual evolutions from Ruyer's *absolute surface of self-overview* and *universe lines of invention*. We also know that most of Ruyer's paradoxes are early formulations of what Laruelle called, in a Marxist-Althusserian manner of speaking, *the Determination in the last instance, i.e* uniduality, or unilateral causality[12].

But Ruyer's Gnosis is above all rather monistic than dualistic, and it consists in a pan-psychism which culminates in solving the psycho-physical parallelism problem out of the quantum mechanics and out of a

[10] Ruyer, Raymond, *Philosophie de la valeur* (Paris : Colin, 1952).

[11] See Hans Jonas, *The Phenomenon of life : towards a philosophical biology* (New York : Dell Pub. Co., 1966).

[12] Raymond Ruyer, *Paradoxes de la conscience et limites de l'automatisme* (Paris : Albin Michel, 1966).

teleological conception of the totipotent embryology[13].

On the contrary, the Gnosis which Laruelle protests to be the heir is precisely the dualistic one, the one that Hans Jonas reproaches to Sartre for being the continuation of, within the Modern Ages[14]. Zorastrians, Sethians, Neoplatonic Hermetists (See A-J Festugières' *Corpus Hermeticum*), Cathars, Anabaptists (See E. Bloch on Müntzer's revolutionary theology), according to Jonas, are sporadic recursive manifestations of a root trend in Thought that has broken in two, even more than History : Reality itself, at its most and deepest ontological level of experience and knowledge.

There lies the archetype of the inmost dualism that decided of the condemnation of Matter, of Flesh, of World, of Existence, of Being. There lies the theoretical decision – that is, the rapture of/in contemplation that decided – on the genuine innocence of

---

[13] See Raymond Ruyer, *Neofinalism* (Minneapolis : University of Minnesota Press, 2016), translated by Alyosha Edlebi ; introduction by Mark B. N. Hansen.

[14] On the difference between Ruyer's and Jonas' responses to Dualism and Gnosis, see Alex Peltier, « D'un corps à son image : Hans Jonas et le modèle rédempteur de la chair », in *Revue Philosophique de Louvain*, Vol 117, 2, May 2019, pp. 341-374.

Human, on its essential immaculate standing in front of the corrupted laws of civilizations, in front of the whole World of intentional manifestation, in front of Being itself and in front of Philosophy *per se*, all of them understood as what Laruelle rigorously calls Hell, and its abusive authoritarian *logos*.

As we can observe, part of this decision, part of this cut, is focused on and brought to the forefront of Laruelle's analyses ; but part is tacit. By following here the Rousseauist lineage of anthropological decision, and by connecting it with the contemporary question of Nihilism and Deconstruction, it is attempted to mark the deep historical continuities that infrastructure Thought, at its inmost radical level.

Some of these continuities can be caught as constructions, or as decisions, as identities or as limits, as differentiations, as discernments, as discriminations, or even as cuts.

One can feel them deep within the main turnings of the philosophical questioning ; and what Laruelle calls « unitary » is the way Philosophy has the pretentiousness to be the answer to the decisions that philosophers grant each time in denial to be the Real, and the way Philosophy comforts itself in synthesis for divisions that have been made up from transcendent, even fascist, unspoken beginnings.

One can feel them when going from the Ancient *Why is there Mistake ?* to the Modern *How is (some) Truth possible ?* ; or when going from the Nietzschean *How to establish immanence ?*, or from the Husserlian *How to establish oneself within immanence ?* to the post-Heideggerian *What use can be made of Trans-cendence ?* Each question lets its axiomatic background echoing, and a very different grounding can be experienced from one to another.

This essay has two cores, which reveal to be a sole one. It follows one historical continuity, inextricably scientific and metaphysical, that questions *the body (of) experience* and its attempted modelizations, as being the lived intersection of meaning and materiality, of syntax and perception, of will and finitude, of glyph and pathos ; and consecutively it investigates François Laruelle's itinerary inside Thought, to explore some genetic steps that have governed the constitution of his non-standard theoretical matrix.

But these two enquiries collide in one when the observation is made that mysteriously the body suddenly vanishes as a thematic at a certain point of Laruelle's writings, although it was a former pivotal axis in the formulation of his thought.

What is at stake is then to elucidate what is assumed to be a decision, the decision to remove *a theoretical lived* out of the crucial articulations which construct the non-philosophical apparatus.

Surely this issue concerns Metaphysics in recent contemporary philosophy, henology and ontology, methodological strictness and structural opportunities of constructivism. But it also involves Physics, Psychiatry, Politics, Linguistics, which are the many domains that Laruelle considers alternatively as having been philosophical attempted authorities over the human mass of the many ones (that) we are, in last analysis.

So from now on History will be getting even faster. There will be a hail of references, of dates, a hailstorm of names and of concepts, of architectures and of visions.

These are the coordinates of a journey that only begins for you – that only begins *at* you. May it be a journey from or may it be a journey towards, this text only indicates what to be passed through, what to be crossed.

The whole landscape to be explored is within, but probably not within the indications lying on the textual page, at least not sufficiently, not even within its voids or its failures. And, as formerly said, nobody, no one, can explore this inner night of indication on your behalf.

Firstly because there is nothing to be explored for the One inside the One. But also because embodied experience is an identity of finitude that can't be explored or experimented from any linguistic statement visually confronted on a plane of paper. At the very least, it is an experience (of) Time, (of) Gramme, (of) Anxiety, (of) Nausea, (of) Vertigo, (of) Reluctance or (of) Indifference. But there is no surrogate for this, while at the same time it is very difficult to assert under which limits it can be said your own.

In the last instance, embodiment can be told as being a pace, a pace of enaction, a pace that seemingly exceeds, overrides, overwhelms the very lines of its determinations. A pace that increases in such a way that only breathlessness can define its inmost lived identity…

Achieved at Puteaux, Paris suburbs,
in June 2023, thanks to S. Degrave

We have to move on.

Isn't it our fate, as the living animalian bodies that we are, destined to grow and to roam – to explore Time and Space ; set to encounter – *via* distal limbs, proximal lips, deep breaths – ; erected to guide ourselves within that strange fluid we call Gravity, and which we feel as the Force that names « Verticality » our in-love relation of adherence with the ground of teeming humus that will absorb our corpse, our form, our trace – just like Death whispers so, in her mono-ideic story, to the inner ears of ours, these ears which listen to angst in a background noise of agony ?

We have to move on… peculiarly when talking about Earth…

Was it at the turn of the ending 19th Western century, or has it already been written in the insights of our highest philosophers in the days that immediately followed Continental Enlightenments ? **Henri Poincaré** (1854-1912) had it recorded in the pages of his epistemology : « For a completely motionless being, there would be neither Space nor geometry. »[15]

And opening our Physiology to non-Euclidian spaces, he added: « Each muscle gives birth to a special sensation likely to increase or to diminish, in such a way that the collection of our muscular sensations will rely on as many variables as many muscles we have. From this point of view, *motor space would have as many dimensions as many muscles we have.* »[16]

[15] Henri Poincaré, *La Valeur de la Science* (Paris : Flammarion, 1911), p. 82.
[16] Henri Poincaré, *La Science et l'Hypothèse* (Paris :

But this was only from a Physics point of view. At the exact same period, Experimental Psychology was erecting out of its classical womb of Philosophy.

In France **Pierre Janet** (1859-1947), immediately followed by **Henri Wallon** (1879-1962) who relayed him in 1937 at his professorial chair in the *Collège de France*, posited that « the psychic unit isn't the anatomized function, it is *a complete act* […] In psychic field, the primitive fact is an agreement, indeed whether successful or failed, it is the essential union between the act and its object. »[17]

This question about unity envelops the problematic of the emergence of the

Flammarion, 1917), p. 73.
[17] Henri Wallon, « Pierre Janet, psychologue réaliste » *Bulletin de psychologie* 14 (184) (1960) : pp. 154-156.

conscious subject from the autonomic reflex activity and from the neurobiological *substratum* that anatomy and histology unveiled at the end of 19th century (the famous struggle between the one-for-two Nobel Priced Cajal and Golgi) : How does the imperceptible transition from motor schemes, « intersecting ones on the others », to the whole of behaviours, provide to « catch the exact moment when the subject is aroused at last […] and when motion has become consciousness ? »[18]

The first reversal, the one implied in the study of this essential unity, and manifested by pragmatic in-situation intelligence rather than operational logical cognition, is the scientific reversal which « substitutes movement for sensations as first elements of psychic life[19]. »

It is the complete reversal of the all introspection psychology : it is the Sensualist statue of Condillac that falls apart. Neither Word nor Sensation : in the beginning was Action[20]. « The presence of the object

---

[18] Henri Wallon, *De L'Acte à la pensée* (Paris : Flammarion, 1970), p. 28.

[19] *Ibid.*, p. 27.

[20] Goethe's readers shall recognize here, barely not disguised, the exact process of translation that Faust gives of John's Gospel in the opening of the *Study Scene*, which will be the scene of the signature of the

prompts to make use of it ; using things personally is a way to identify them before any objective identification. »[21]

This new approach of the roots of Thought, that puts actions prior to representations, H. Wallon shares it with Jean Piaget : « Actually the perceptive field is essentially an action field... » ; but he goes further : « Action, depending on its level, is more or less able to discern or to redesign the structures [of the perceptive field]. It integrates to them more or less numerous circumstances, more or less diverse, or opportune ones. It ordinates them in the direction of its own needs, and it results in a more or less quick solution. It doesn't assemble anything without melting it into its own unity. It acts like a constellating force, each element having sense only inside the situation created by it. »[22]

This Situationist understanding of expe-

pact with Mephistopheles. Then Faust translates then *the Word* into *Sense*, before he understands it as *Force*, and finally, confident in the Spirit which supports him, he writes : *Im Anfang war die Tat*. Who wouldn't already discern here a biblical prefiguration of John Langshaw Austin's theses on performative utterance, or at least Fichte's *Tathandlung* ?

[21] *Ibid.*, p. 60.

[22] *Ibid.*, p. 70.

rience (in a very different meaning, we have to be careful of this, than the usual meaning of being more influenced by external factors than by internal ones), Wallon would impart it to Maurice Merleau-Ponty (1908-1961), especially when Merleau-Ponty composed his teaching about child development. And Existentialism would hand it over to **Guy Debord** (1931-1994) when trying to make, out of urban drifting, a real deep art of creating situations ; but it would also somehow transmit it to Structuralism, especially *via Gestalt psychologie.*

In Germany, the 19th century nascent Psychology was dealing with more down-to-earth questions, but leading to the very grounds of embodiment. **Wilhelm Wundt** (1832-1920), accomplishing his masters' breakthroughs in Psychophysics, **Gustav**

Fechner (1801-1887) and **Ernst Weber** (1795-1878), having laid the foundations for any inquiries about sensations sources and sensations organs, a question was remaining, more and more searing as Psychology was accumulating data, the question of how different sources and modalities of sensations could come to a unified experience of the World, could come to an evidence of the self as being one.

This question of the unification of the internal experience was especially an inheritance from Aristippus of Cyrene (435 BC-356 BC) whose disciples used to talk about an « inner touch » (Cicero's *Tactus Intimus*[23]).

Montaigne (1533-1592) has this charming way to tell : « The Cyrenayans held that nothing was perceptible outwardly, and only that was perceivable which by the *inward fondling*, like pain and delight… »[24]

During a long period, at least from Aristotle, external senses weren't believed to get to the inner sense (which was equal to consciousness) if not having been purified first by the « common sense » (*koinon aistheterion*)[25].

But at the heart of Enlightenments, an unheralded and nowadays barely unknown thinker, **Joseph-Adrien Lelarge de Lignac** (1710-1762), probably the 18th century's philosopher who went the deepest in exploring his intimate being (putting aside Rousseau who knew better how to adorn and garland his introspection with vivid details and contingent anecdotes), while he was looking into *the pure*

[23] Cicero, *Academica*, II, 24.
[24] Michel de Montaigne, *Essays*, Book II, Chapter XII : « The Apology of Raymond Segond. »
[25] Aristotle, *De Anima*, III, 2.

intimate sense (when our soul, released from any external, lets itself fall into a state of dreaminess where only remains the feeling of its being), pointed towards what he named *the sense of coexistence of our body*[26].

Encyclopædists like Turgot or d'Alembert, both under the Sensualist influence of John Locke, followed suit and began to talk about an *inner tact*[27].

But the most durable term, destined to play a major role in Science, especially in Neurology and Psychiatry, would come from a

[26] Joseph-Adrien Lelarge de Lignac, *Éléments de Métaphysique tirés de l'Expérience : Lettres à un Matérialiste* (Paris : Desaint & Saillant, 1753), « Sixth letter », p.100 *sqq.*
[27] See *Encyclopædia of Diderot and d'Alembert* : « Existence ».

German physician **Johann Christian Reil** (1759-1813) who first used in 1794 the noun *cœnæsthesia* to name the *Gemeingefühl*, the general sensibility which integrates all sensitive afferences in one global body feeling of ease or unease, depending on health condition and on attention.

This distinction would be taken up by **Carl Wernicke** (1848-1905) questioning our *somato-psyche* or by **Sir Charles Scott Sherrington** (1857-1952) exploring models for our *interoception* and *proprioception*.

But above all cœnæsthesia would become a central concept in Psychopathology, opening all along the 19th century possibilities to catch troubles like *cœnæsthopathy* (Dupré & Camus), *hysteria* (Ribot & Sollier) or *depersonalization* and *melancholic negation delusion* (Séglas), leading to the major contribution to Psychopathology built by **Charles Blondel** (1876-1939) : *La Conscience morbide*[28].

According to Blondel cœnæsthesia defines the experience of the *pure psychological* (never accessible from outside of consciousness, unconceptualized in normal state) that brings unity and real continuity to our conscious life,

---

[28] Charles Blondel, *The Troubled Conscience and the Insane Mind* (UK-Abington : Routledge, 2014). But we can also refer to German E. Berrios & F. Fuentenebro. « Charles Blondel and *La Conscience Morbide* », in *History of Psychiatry* 8, 30 Pt 2 (1997), pp. 277-295.

the visceral lived experience on which would lay the *perceptive faith* called by Merleau-Ponty[29].

Facing Wundt as his opponent in modelizing experimental Psychology was **Carl Stumpf** (1848-1936).

Stumpf was, just like Alexius Meinong (1853-1920), one of Franz Brentano's students (1838-1917). Stumpf and Wundt were struggling around the process of *Fusion (Verschmelzung)*, especially about the fusion of tonal sensation when listening to music.

---

[29] See Eugen Minkowski, *Traité de Psychopathologie* (Paris : PUF, 1966 ; Le Plessis-Robinson : Les empêcheurs de penser en rond, 1999), pp. 516-547. In Minkowski's treaty, Blondel's cœnæsthesia is compared to Pierre Janet's *sense of real* and *function of presentification*.

And when **Edmund Husserl** (1859-1938) decided, after hearing Brentano's teaching, to devote completely his life to Philosophy, he went to Halle under the supervision of Stumpf in order to prepare his *Habilitationsschrift*; he would dedicate his second work, *Logische Untersuchungen*, laying the foundations of Phenomenology, to this important master of his.

What Husserl's early works were about, were the problem of *continuity* and the grasp of singularities as identical to themselves (different to others) and simultaneously connected to the whole group — when counting arithmetical elements and quantities. A situation of *distinguishing oneself while simultaneously not being distinguished*, about what we will have to talk again and to think further in the following pages.

To lead these researches, Husserl would use two major concepts : *fusion*, on one hand, which he had received from Stumpf, and *Gestalt* (form), on the other hand, which he had taken from **Ernst Mach** (1838-1916), the same way Christian von Ehrenfels (1859-1932) would take it from, at the same time[30].

Ernst Mach was one of the central scientific characters of this period. Preparing the overstepping of the notion of an absolute space, Kantian-like, while working on redefining the inertia reference frame, Mach partook of exporting into Psychology the concept of *field* from electro-magnetic physics, as put in equations by **James Clerk Maxwell** (1831-1879)[31].

---

[30] Carlo Ierna, « Husserl et Stumpf sur la *Gestalt* et la fusion », *Philosophiques* 362 (2009), pp. 489-510.

[31] See Gilbert Simondon, *L'Individuation psychique et*

His intensive experimental activity on senses led Mach to modelize how postural balance integrates on motricity all vectors from other senses – *i.e.* around verticality and the living experience of gravity, that is : of Earth.

Obsessed as they are by how to explain what phenomenological Reduction is, historians of philosophy have focused too much on Husserl's difference between objective body and living flesh (*Körper/Leib*), and it has become a platitude of our embodiment Phenomenology.

But we have neglected to tell and teach the rich way in which Husserl established how

collective à la lumière des notions de forme et d'information (Grenoble : Jérôme Millon, 2005), pp. 537-58.

kinæsthesia, the immanent muscles and joints sense of the motions of our body, intervenes as a « knot constituting World » ; and how kinestheses and motivation relations between *Æstheta* build the apprehension of the Thing, and prepare the emergence of causality connections[32].

When **Wolfgang Köhler** (1887-1967) took over the directorship of the *Psychological Institute of Berlin* from his teacher Carl Stumpf, the project of his research team (including Kurt Koffka, Max Wertheimer, and Kurt Lewin)

[32] Edmund Husserl, *Ideas Pertaining to a Pure Phenomenology and to a Phenomenological Philosophy – Second Book : Studies in the Phenomenology of Constitution*, trans. R. Rojcewicz and A. Schuwer (Dordrecht : Kluwer, 1989), pp. 60-95.

was « to resolve the problems posed by the Husserlian phenomenology by means of an experimental type of scientific psychology that drew upon the concepts of quantum mechanics (Köhler having studied physics with Planck as well), particularly that of *field*. »[33] The 1920's *Gestalt* psychology was born, especially exposed to struggle against Pavlov's atomistic psychology, on the question of linear neural causality to explain consciousness[34].

Their ambition to discover the laws of immediate experience, the experience that we have of things and meanings as organized wholes – what Husserl initially called « figural moments »[35] –, would be a major support of

[33] Jean-Pierre Dupuy, « Philosophy and Cognition : Historical Roots, » in : Jean Petitot, Francisco J. Varela, Bernard Pachoud, and Jean-Michel Roy, eds., *Naturalizing Phenomenology – Issues in Contemporary Phenomenology and Cognitive Science* (Stanford, CA : Stanford University Press, 1999), pp. 539-58.

[34] About these epistemological struggles, see the amazingly sharp Erwin Straus, *The Primary World of Senses : A Vindication of Sensory Experience*, trans. J. Needleman (London : Collier-Macmillan Ltd., 1963).

[35] Edmond Husserl, *Philosophy of Arithmetic: Psychological and Logical Investigations* with Supplementary Texts from 1887-1901, in : Edmund Husserl : *Collected Works*, vol. 10, ed. Rudolf Bernet (Dordrecht : Kluwer, 2003).

the theory of *Body Schema*, formulated in 1911 by **Henry Head** (1861-1940) and **Gordon Morgan Holmes** (1876-1965)[36].

When talking about embodiment, if there is one concept to be saved from complete oblivion among scientific models, exhumed out of the typical late 19th century research, we can be pretty sure this is the concept of *Body Schema*.

It is the quintessential extract of an inter-disciplinary era gathering outstandingly vivid knowledge and research fields that had scatte-red with the European collapse of World War 1.

We can even assert, on the testimony of what we grasped from Husserl's works in the second book of his *Ideas…*, that the *Crisis of European Sciences* which he confronted in the

[36] H. Head & G. M. Holmes, « Sensory disturbances from cerebral lesions », *Brain*, 34 (1911), pp. 102-254.

1930's, was the crisis of a Body Schema, the Body Schema of a continental civilization – a crisis following its lack, or its loss, of a living own body of experience – even though Husserl neared it and explained it from the Galilean geometrical point of view[37].

Sketched by neurologists such as **Jean-Martin Charcot** (1825-1893) ; baptized, with an exquisite Kantian conceptual sensibility, by the psychiatrist and otologist **Pierre Bonnier** (1861-1918) who first talked about « *schemata* of the motor function » and who designed the pathological portrait of *aschematia* to describe cœnestopathies characterized with symptoms of inadequate representations of the space when occupied by some part of the body[38] – the Body Schema rose at the crossroad of

[37] Edmond Husserl, *The Crisis of European Sciences and Transcendental Philosophy*, trans. D. Carr (Evanston : Northwestern University Press, 1970).
[38] Pierre Bonnier, « L'Aschématie », *Revue Neurologique*, 13 (1905), pp. 605-609.

Physiology, Histology, Neurology, Psychology, Psychiatry, Sociology, Anthropology, early Psycho-analysis, and it can be felt as the axis of psycho-somatics, whether of hysteria or of hypnosis.

The Image and Appearance of the Human Body, **Paul Ferdinand Schilder**'s summa (1886-1940), figures the 1930's *paragon* of this scientific construction, which can be valued, as a scientific piece of art, like the Eiffel Tower is, as an engineering accomplishment[39].

Body schema's conceptual decline would begin in the 1960's, with the epistemological secession of the post-Lacanian psychoanalysis and the refusal to mix anymore physiological data and symbolical libidinal investment (*cathexis*). We find a perfect illustration of this in Françoise Dolto's conceptual split (1908–1988) between Body Schema (zoo-anthropolo-

[39] Paul Schilder, *The Image and appearance of the human body : studies in the constructive energies of the psyche* (London : K. Paul, Trench, Trubner, 1935).

gical) and Unconscious Image of the body (personnal)[40].

But in the meantime this concept was playing a priceless role in Merleau-Ponty's thought, as the recent analyses of his manuscripts and the re-reading of his work has shown ; especially by articulating a prenoetic mode of knowledge through postural impregnation[41] ; while two astonishing figureheads of Psycho-analysis were leading breakthroughs inside embodiment and early motor construction of psyche :

Donald Winnicott (1896-1971) – with his autonomous psychoanalytic work on *holding* and *handling* as primary relation with the newborn ;

[40] Françoise Dolto, *L'Image inconsciente du corps* (Paris : Éditions du Seuil, 1984).

[41] Emmanuel de Saint Aubert, *Être et chair I : Du corps au désir : l'habilitation ontologique de la chair* [Being and Flesh I : from body to desire : the flesh ontological enablement] (Paris : Vrin, 2013).

and **Julian de Ajuriaguerra** (1911-1993) – intriguing figure of French pædiatric psychiatry, famous for having led literary experiments with mescaline, and who constructed new therapy methods involving relaxation techniques (Schultz's autogenic training, Jacobson's Biofeedback, Alexander's Eutony) and bodily mediated psychoanalysis, on the basis of Henri Wallon's *tonal-emotional dialogue* ; in such an extent that his work finally drove to create a new profession : Psychomotrician[42].

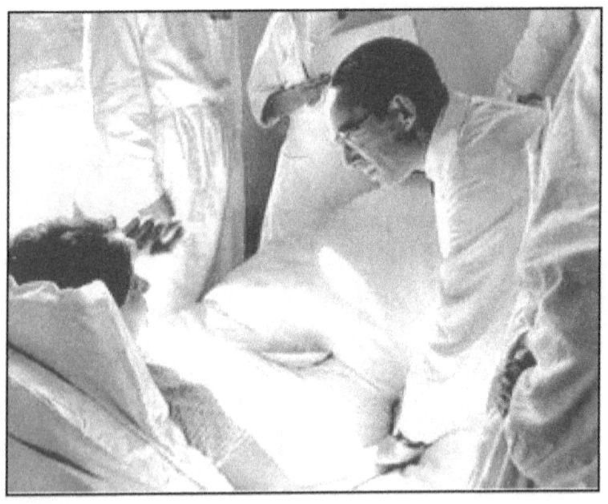

[42] Julian de Ajuriaguerra, *La Naissance de la psychomotricité*, 4 Volumes, A. Berthoz, F. Joly & G. Labes, eds. (Paris : Papyrus, 2009).

As Macdonald Critchley (1900-1997) partook of pointing out, Body Schema was too much of a conceptual umbrella[43], confusing unconscious physiological processes and representational images build inside social interactions.

It has taken decades to discern how such a concept could carry yet solid perspectives in modelization, and we can still see nowadays someone like **Shaun Gallagher** (1848-) struggling to clarify the misunderstandings involved in this inter-disciplinary notion, in order to save what could be the most promising trail when it comes to filling the famous « explanatory gap » between objective

[43] R. Angelergues, D. Anzieu, E. Boesch, Y. Brès, J.-B. Pontalis, R. Zazzo, *Psychologie de la connaissance de soi* (Paris : Presses Universitaires de France, 1975).

quantified descriptions and experienced *qualia*[44].

Actually, only « body » or « embodiment » could be trickier concepts, as much as being even wider and exposed as such to deeper confusions. But to get to Gallagher's contemporary summa, *How body shapes the mind*[45], scientific backstage labour had to be performed first.

[44] Joseph Levine, « Materialism and qualia : The explanatory gap », *Pacific Philosophical Quaterly* 64 (1983), p. 354.
[45] Shaun Gallagher, *How the Body Shapes the Mind* (New York : Oxford University Press, 2005).

What happened to Body Schema is that it had to succeed through the ordeal of Falsification, thanks to **Karl Popper** (1902-1994). And this wasn't anymore a matter of theory and large modelizations, but a matter of lab work and experimental details, *i.e.* a matter of small articles publications rather than *summæ*.

On these ways **Jacques Paillard** (1920-2006) conducted a 50 years model career in Psychophysics, from 1940's electromyography experiments on proprioception, resulting in his PhD dissertation[46], to our contemporary familiar fMRI exploration of brain activity : more than 250 dispersed publications leading to the acknowledgement of a necessary physiological distinction between body schema and body image[47].

But Paillard's researches may interest the thought of embodiment at a deeper theoretical level.

Keeping up with Poincaré's insight, Paillard explored the question of embodied spatial

---

[46] Jacques Paillard, *Réflexes et régulations d'origine proprioceptive chez l'Homme. Étude neuro-physiologique et psycho-physiologique*, Thèse de Doctorat ès Sciences, Paris-Sorbonne. Série A 2858 N° 3729. (Paris : Librairie Arnette, 1955).

[47] Jacques Paillard, « Vectorial *versus* configural encoding of body space : a neural basis for a distinction between Body schema and Body image. » in Helena De Preester & Veroniek Knockaert, eds., *Body Image and Body Schema* (Amsterdam : John Benjamins, 2005), pp. 62-89. Thanks to the Web Archives, traces of Jacques Paillard's complete works has been saved :
https://web.archive.org/web/20070819011120fw_/
http://jacquespaillard.apinc.org/jpbibli48-60.html

frames of reference[48]. Far from images and representational consciousness of space, Paillard's statement is that object locations « can be coded in terms of the movement required to get from one [location] to the other », the *sensorimotor* mode of processing spatial information generating and storing its own neural mapping of space (different from and coexisting with the representational mode).

This sensorimotor mode concerns that part of the physical world to which the organism is attuned, as we saw above, by action, building constellations of meanings in-situation : an *Umwelt* of intervening inside the sensitive world.

[48] Jacques Paillard, « Motor and representational framing of space. » in J. Paillard, ed., *Brain and Space*, chap. 10 (Oxford : Oxford University Press, 1991), pp. 163-182.

Using mathematical topology, Paillard describes the sensorimotor space like *a spatial structure of paths*, embodying trajectories of reaching which construct our peripersonal space motor experience.

Spatial reality to which organisms accede depending on their sensorial equipment, the exercise of motricity contributes to transform the sensitive field caught by sense organs.

The acting body calls out space around itself, and each perceptive modality divides physical reality in a plurality of spaces accorded to functions (retinocentric visuo-motor space, lips and mouth touching and tasting space, hands and fingers grasping and caressing space…).

The dialogue of these local spaces results in the coalescence of an architected sensori-motor territory of existence, unified by interlocked proprioceptive floors which correspond with anatomical motor segments (ocular orbits-cephalic-neck axis, shoulder-elbow-wrist segments, feet-ankles-knees-hip pendulums…).

This configurational space of living vectors, mapped in our active motricity, shapes an egocentric spatial frame of reference on which our multimodal perceptive experience of World relies.

In that psychophysical field, Paillard's works have opened the way to experiments on proprioception and the revealing of the dependence of our senses on the global muscular and conjunctive sensitive structures (golgi tendon organs and muscle spindles), in such an extent that it could provoke perceptive illusions and motor hallucinations[49].

Paillard's works thus confirm **Michel Henry** (1922-2002) when rendering Maine de Biran's statement that the immediate and non-constituted feeling of effort and action, our affective experience of the « resisting continuum », structures our perception and our consciousness[50].

[49] See Mikael Bergenheim, Édith Ribot-Ciscar & Jean-Pierre Roll, « Proprioceptive population coding of two-dimensional limb movements in humans, » *Exp Brain* Res 134 (2000) : PP. 301-21.
[50] Michel Henry, *Philosophy and Phenomenology of the Body*, trans. G. Etzkorn (The Hague : Nijhoff, 1975).

But they also prepare the developments of contemporary models for neural anticipation of perception through action, like *pre-motor tonal attitude* which increases motor efficiency[51] ; and doing so these works contribute to the deep philosophical contemporary interests in « Naturalizing Phenomenology » with the recourse of neurosciences[52].

Nevertheless Paillard's propositions are intriguing at a different level of capacity.

Not only working with mathematical tools but also involving semiotics in his researches[53], the relational totality which Paillard explored as a unified segmented motor mapping experience that organizes our existential activity, he expressly rendered it as a *structure of space-language*, as an *immanent topology* of interlocked segments in the constant process of building our environment of possibilities and meanings for action.

---

[51] Alain Berthoz and Jean-Luc Petit, *The Physiology and Phenomenology of Action*, trans. C. Macann (2006; Oxford : Oxford University Press, 2008).

[52] Varela *et alii, op.cit.* (see note 33).

[53] Jacques Paillard (et alii.), *Les Unités sémiotiques temporelles. Éléments nouveaux d'analyse musicale* (Marseille : Documents Musurgia, Diffusion MIM, 1996).

Contrary to our usual habits, what Paillard has built is a structural biosemiotics, rooted in our biological corporeity as a permanent interpretative activity through motor functions.

Such a non-linguistic Structuralism may surprise us because we have recorded that Structuralism was both under the influence of linguistics, especially of **Ferdinand de Saussure** (1857-1913), of Psychoanalysis, especially because of the development of its notion of unconscious, and of Russian materialist Formalism, above all within the influence of **Roman Jakobson** (1896- 1982).

But it is just as if we had forgotten that *Gestalt Theorie* was the cradle of Structuralism.

Indeed, even if superficially enclosed in the era of industrialised press, which has brought to its climax the Post-Romantic influence of literary figures (artist characters culminating as the only survival and remaining hope of the unleashed rationalism society that has sunk by leading 19th century to World War 1), the modalities of 1960's Structuralism were above all extensions of what Existentialists have broadcasted from *Gestalt theoryie* especially Merleau-Ponty *via* his teachings, with his first book : *The Structures of behaviour*[54], and also when publishing, for example, **Kurt Goldstein** (1878-1965) in Gallimard's Philosophical series, which Merleau-Ponty was director of[55].

[54] Maurice Merleau-Ponty, *The Structure of Behavior*, trans. A. L. Fisher (1942 ; Boston : Beacon Press, 1963 ; London : Methuen, 1965).
[55] Kurt Goldstein, *La Structure de l'organisme : intro-*

But moreover we have to remember that the French translator of **Victor von Weizsäcker**'s *Der Gestaltkreis* (1886-1957) was Michel Foucault (1926-1984), who was also involved in publishing Existentialist Psychiatry in his early works[56]: Foucault symptomatically chose to translate *Gestalt* into *Structure*, not into *Form*[57].

It is quite difficult for us to imagine, because continental societies have been so much over-turned since then, but we have to retrace that from the late 19th century until 1970's when television grew worldwide, the only massively expanded private contact with

duction à la biologie à partir de la pathologie humaine (Der Aufbau des Organismus) (Paris : Gallimard, 1951).

[56] Ludwig Binswanger, *Rêve et existence*, introduction by Michel Foucault (Paris : Desclée de Brouwer, 1954).

[57] Viktor Von Weizsäcker, *Le Cycle de la structure : Der Gestaltkreis*, trans. Michel Foucault and Daniel Rocher (1933 ; Paris : Desclée de Brouwer, 1958).

fictions and narrative arts was literature, and radio, which had its golden age in the 1950's.

Louis-Ferdinand Céline (1894-1961) has amazingly depicted in his childhood fictionalized souvenirs, *Death on Credit*[58], how Rationalism has become a lucrative publishing business and Technoscience a popular entertainment : paper printed careers were the back-in-the-days star system. Sartre, Beauvoir, Camus… were as famous, popular and influent names as Juliette Gréco (singer), Django Reinhardt (musician) or Gérard Philippe (actor).

So, if we except the fascinating character that was **René Daumal** (1908-1944) (whose Avant-garde poetry and experimental Meta-

---

[58] Louis-Ferdinand Céline, *Death on Credit* (*Mort à credit* ; a.k.a *Death on the Installment Plan*) (1936 ; tr. by John H. P. Marks, Boston : Little, Brown and Company, 1938).

physics led to a high level of body practice in the wake of Gurdjieff (1866?-1949) but whose death happened too early when his intellectual influence in France was as promising as Sartre's was) ; or if we except the better-known **Antonin Artaud** (1896-1948) whose theatrical ontology of cruelty was supported by a *pathos* and breathing work, and has led to the crucial conceptualization of *Body-without-organs* – it was obviously old-established that an intellectual career has very few to do with body, but rather with discourse, *Logos* and ultimately, as a scientific awareness form of analytic and critical knowledge, with logology.

If we didn't have the examples of Jacques Paillard, or of the Esalen Institute where *Gestalt* practice was related to massage, or body-mind interventions, since 1964 under the influence of **Fritz Perls** (1893-1970), we couldn't be able to catch how Structuralism could have initially something to do with the body, with embodiment, motor function, topology of carnal consciousness, even if this is clearly something that has been lost along the way of Structuralism's rising influence.

Lost in such an extent after Foucault reduced clinical arts, psychiatric cares and prophylactic political concerns into mere discourses to be judged outside of any intentions, outside of any lived feelings, outside of any intersubjective relationships, in the name of the materialistic metholodology relying on the only immanent Text, just like only from a librarian point of view summing up generations from his leathery desk[59];

[59] We can compare Foucault's *The Birth of the Clinic*, trans. A. Sheridan Smith (1963; New York:

after **Roland Barthes'** (1915-1980) reducing of motivations into mythologies and Gérard Genette's (1930-2018) generalisation of Palympsest ; after **Jacques Lacan**'s (1901-1981) cessation of considering energetic in favour of Matheme[60]; after **Louis Althusser**'s (1918-1990) Marxist privilege for epistemology at the expense of individual experience[61]... lost in such an extent that, when Post-Structuralism began to rise, especially in the form of **Jacques Derrida**'s (1930-2004) De-construction, there were only remains of texts, discourses, rhetoric, grammar, linguistics, to be concerned about, but no more any body – no body anymore...

Pantheon Books, 1973 ; London : Tavistock Publications Ltd, 1976) and *History of Madness* (1961 ; New York : Routledge, 2006) with Georges Canguilhem's *The Normal and the Pathological*, trans. C. R. Fawcett (1943 ; New York : Zone Books, 1991) and Paul Bercherie's *Les Fondements de la Clinique vol. 1 : Histoire et Structure du Savoir Psychiatrique* (Paris : Seuil 1980 ; L'Harmattan, 2004), in order to catch the differences of posture regarding to discourses and praxes, differences that Gladys Swain's (1945-1993) books have also emphasized.

[60] See Paul Ricœur, *Freud and Philosophy : An Essay on Interpretation*, trans. D. Savage (1965 ; New Haven : Yale University Press, 1970).

[61] See Michel Henry, *Marx : A Philosophy of Human Reality*, trans. K. McLaughlin (1976 ; Bloomington : Indiana University Press, 1983).

Beyond the luxury of antimetaboles which this generation was peculiarly generous in the use of, it is always difficult not to smile when imaging Derrida as he was browsing pages and pages of Husserl while writing *Speech and Phenomena*, looking into the text and endlessly asking « where is the living present ? Where is the living present ? I can't see it anywhere... » ; there sure wasn't any living own body, any kinæstheses, any embodied *pathos* to be found among letters ; and even the metaphorical use of language as essence of philosophical thought could have been defined very differently than it was posit in *Margins of Philosophy* to confront Ontology and Conceptuality[62].

[62] We can see and compare Jacques Derrida, « White Mythology : Metaphor in the Text of Philosophy » in *Margins – of Philosophy*, trans. A. Bass (1972 ; Chicago : Chicago University Press, 1982) with Paul Ricœur, *The Rule of Metaphor*, trans. R. Czerny (1975 ; Toronto : University of Toronto press, 1977) to catch the gap that Saussurianism has let inside French

We certainly can find some organic traces in Derrida's use of the Nietzschean process of Genealogy, when digging into origins to erect their primary dispersion, like *force* versus *form* in *Writing and Difference*, but even the living own proper body was always already there to attest (rather than immediate affection of one's agency or structural motor space of one's situation) dispossession, impropriety, raptus of speech by an evil God...[63]

It is clearly *different*, if we can allow ourselves to say so, when talking about **Gilles Deleuze** (1925-1995), even if he was rather preoccupied by Philosophy, History of thought and conceptual assemblages than interested in actual experiences of embodiment ; and even if the *Body-without-organ* is rather a conceptual character used to explain a plane of syntaxes and causalities than a rooting to be deepen inside self Event and Becoming.

theorisation of meaning, reference, logic, propositions, semantics.

[63] Jacques Derrida, « Force and signification », « La Parole soufflée » and « The Theatre of cruelty and the closure of representation, » in *Writing and Difference*, trans. A. Bass (1967 ; Chicago : University of Chicago Press, 1978).

At least Deleuze philosophical landscape is fulfilled with breasts and mouths, connected with hesitating anus. At least his desert is scattered with dismembered limbs or trans-fixed visages, his continuities are spoken from intimate flux of secretions, of urines, fæces, saliva, sperm, mucus, cyprine. At least his Unity without representation bears the name given to flesh when undivided and when welcoming partial, transitional, fractioned located functions.

Though imaginary and mostly uniquely metaphorical masks, literary composed clothes for transcendental machines about which multiplying variations and effects, Deleuzian contents retain some thematic materials from Baruch Spinoza (1632-1677), from Friedrich

Nietzsche (1844-1900), from **Henri Bergson** (1859-1941) or from **Raymond Ruyer** (1902–1987), related to carnal lived experiences which sustain a residual imaginary atmosphere of embodiment inside his demonstrations.

And above all, Deleuze maintains a dynamic and profound sensibility to Situations, to complex assemblages of processes of signification interwoven with action and semantic behaviours.

Ultimately Situations are precisely what Deleuze asks philosophers to be able to invent under the name of *Concepts*, but excluding *Percepts* and *Affects* to be direct concerns for philosophical production.

Metaphorically or not, reducing phenomenological intuition, consciousness and intentionality, to only Text, in the way Derrida played his theoretical move, was more alike to an intensification of Structuralism rather than a bypassing.

By formally and materially reducing immanence to its textual contents and architecture, Derrida was perfectly fitted to the obsession of the moment with linguistics, narratology, formalist novels[64]; and what he was accomplishing was the process of determining all phenomenological regions of Being under the spectrum of a single one.

If all that appears is only Text, if all that proceeds is only syntax and grammar of traces, then body, embodiment, carnal experience, entrenchment in flesh, are put apart, under the hierarchy of literature and words.

We can easily understand why Michel Henry, haunted by a non-representational embodied experience of Ipseity outside of any ontological monism, *i.e.* outside of any kind of Difference, any Phenomenological distance,

---

[64] There is deep consistency for his firsts essays to be published in *Tel quel*, Philippe Sollers' Review (where figureheads of *Nouveau Roman* and Structuralism, such as the amazing Jean Thibaudeau (1935-2013) for novel or Denis Roche (1937-2015) for poetry, were occupying a prominent place) as well as his first books to be edited next by les Éditions de Minuit which were founders of the *Nouveau Roman* movement in the mid 50th.

any transcendental gap, wasn't very keen on those Parisianisms and preferred building is œuvre at the very opposite of the country rather than being exposed to such a theoretical context of conspiracy against the body[65].

The superficial interest of Foucault in the utopian body, which has always been rather an occasion to sadistic complaisant depictions of power and cruelty[66], doesn't open to any deeper descriptions either, unless filtered by

[65] Henry's awarded novel, *L'Amour les yeux fermés* (Paris : Gallimard, 1976), is pretty explicit about what he felt concerning this generation of Parisian thought, especially regarding to the academic events of May 1968. The way Lacan tried to deride Henry's Thesis, *The Essence of Manifestation,* when it was published (1963 ; The Hague: Nijhoff, 1973, trans. G. Etzkorn), can draw the basis of this impossibility for the Structuralist generation to hear any fundamental construction about embodiment and the feeling of conspiracy that Henry's nowadays readers can complain about (see for instance the interview between Mikkel Borsh-Jacobsen and Chris Oakley in Todd Dufresne (Ed.), *Returns of the "French Freud" : Freud, Lacan, and Beyond* (New York : Routledge, 1997) ; Lacan quotes Michel Henry without even naming him in the last text from *Écrits*: « Science and Truth » (1966, p. 870 ; New York : W.W. Norton & Co., 2006, p. 739).

[66] On this matter, the opening of Michel Foucault, *Discipline and Punish : the Birth of the Prison*, A. Sheridan (1975 ; New York: Random House, 1977) is explicitly symptomatic of his sadistic personal tastes.

political priorities rather than leading to any theory, ontology or genetic approach of embodiment.

These observations are also particularly visible in **François Laruelle**'s itinerary (1937-).

When considering the first step of his work, *i.e.* the period which he numbered Philosophy 1, that lasts from 1974 – year he defended his unpublished PhD Thesis: *Economy of the effects-of-Being* – to 1981 – year he published *The minority principle* (his very first attempt to veer out of philosophical manners of reaching immanence by using means of transcendence, and his entrance into Philosophy 2, Non-Philosophy's ground zero)[67] –, the body, the semantic field of embodiment and the carnal lived materiality were widely at function in Laruelle set of thought.

What seems obvious in his writing at this period is that every conceptual occurrence of body (*Body-without-beings, Body-of-Being, Body-of-Writing, Textual Body, Libido of inscription, materiality of political body, immanent inscription of drives on the body of the unconscious, undifferantiated full/plane body, aphoristic body, Body-of-the-Other,*

[67] François Laruelle, *Le Principe de minorité* [*The Minority Principle*] (Paris: Aubier Montaigne, 1981).

Nietzschean immediate hand-to-hand affirmation of fascism, Body of Eternal Recurrence of the Same, set-to-Body, Body-for-positions, intensive libidinal process of textual production, Body for Multiplicities, a-signifying Body, Body specified as æsthetic form of desire possibilities, fractional organs of Power, intensive body, topological body of Libido…) is explicitly some extraction from Deleuze's conceptual matrices (or at the very least Nietzsche's). And for a good reason…

Laruelle's early problematic was to graft *Anti-Œdipus* on *Glas (Clang)*, to transplant, or even implant, Deleuze's *Intensive Repetition* inside Derrida's *Deconstructionist Writing* — his initial question being to exhibit how Metaphysics represses its transcendental need for an engine of Otherness as a function in its own economy of movement and becoming — for instance, in *Textual Machines*, the question of what energetic libido drives the Deconstructor at labour, at leading « the only process which transforms with its materials and which consumes on-the-spot to go further »[68].

But from that moment onwards, *i.e.* from the very moment he started to build an approach accorded to the One, even when analysing Deleuze's idealistic infinite Difference in 1986 and confronting it with Derrida's aporetic Judaism of realistic finite Differance[69], the body has vanished from Laruelle's conceptual spectrum.

The body barely outcrops only under the aspect of *cadaverization* when talking about the structural moment of the deconstructing process that « conjugates cadaverization with vivifying affirmation », in continuity with the Double Bind ; a strucutral moment that Laruelle calls *Body-without-writing*, using Deleuze's *plane of immanence* to characterize Derrida specific Judaism[70].

[68] François Laruelle, *Machines textuelles* (Paris : Seuil, 1976), p. 14. A translation of the Introduction, by T. Adkins, is available on line at: http://speculativeheresy.wordpress.com/2013/09/01/translation-of-f-laruelles-introduction-to-textual-machines/
[69] François Laruelle, *Philosophies of Difference : A Critical Introduction to Non-Philosophy*, trans. R. Gangle (1986 ; New York : Continuum 2010).
[70] *Ibid.*, p. 130.

We can henceforth only feel the 90's concept of *Cloning*, axiomatized in *The Principles of Non-Philosophy*, as distantly echoing with something related to the body. But nothing like Flesh, Embodiment, even like Incarnation, makes any appearance anymore, though heretically coming to talk of Christ and Mystics[71].

One interesting recent change, concerning what Laruelle calls the non-philosophical *posture* (*i.e.* a motor attitude) : its *stance* – has led to the sudden and unexpected reappearance of body inside the discourse of Non-Standard Thought, in 2013 :

> « Before the eye, the hand, the torso are implicated in [photography], perhaps it is from the most obscure and the most irreflexive depth of the body that the photographic act departs. Not from the organ-body or body as organ-support, from the substance-body, but from a body absolutely without organs, from a stance rather than a position. The photographer does not throw himself into the World ; he

[71] François Laruelle, *Future Christ : A Lesson in Heresy*, trans. A. P. Smith (2002 ; New York : Continuum 2010)] and *Mystique non-philosophique à l'usage des contemporains* [*Non-Philosophical Mysticism for Contemporaries' Use*] (Paris : L'Harmattan, 2007).

replaces himself firstly in his body as in a stance, and renounces all corporeal or psychic intentionality. « Stance » – this word means : to be rooted in oneself, to be held within one's own immanence, to be at one's station rather than in a position relative to the « motif ». If there is a photographic thinking, it is first and foremost of the order of a feeling of one's naive self rather than of the decision, of auto-impression rather than of expression, of the self-inherence of the body rather than of being-in-the-World. A thinking that is rooted in rather than upon a corporeal base. What is the body as photographic base, stripped of intentionality ? It is that which concentrates in itself an undivided and precisely non-intentional vision-force. What body for photography? Precisely not the phenome-nological body as part of the World or as thrown-into-the-World, but an originary and transcendental arche-body that is, from the outset, « vision » through and through ; but an as-yet un-objectivating vision.[…] The existence of the photographer does not precede his essence ; it is his body as force, indivisible into organs, that precedes the World. […] if there is a type of intentionality peculiar to photography, if it no longer directs itself towards the World, but only supports itself upon it, it does so, no doubt, so as to frame a universal shot which belongs rather to objective fiction. This reduction is that of a stance, and is assured by the lived-body in the most subjective or immanent of manners. Not by a rational or bloodless subject, or indeed one reduced, for example, to an eye ; but by a body as absolute, uncircumventable requisite of the photographic act. »[72]

The craftsmanship which every reader can recognize immediately at functioning behind well identified conceptual patterns, is Deleuze's and Henry's, respectively within the « body absolutely without organs » and within « the self-inherence of the body [...] undivided [...] originary and transcendental arche-body [...] that precedes the World [...] the lived-

[72] François Laruelle, *The Concept of Non-Photography (Bilingual edition)*, trans. R. Mackay (Falmouth : Urbanomic/New York : Sequence, 2013), pp. 12-14 ; minor variations are introduced in the translation.

body in the most subjective or immanent of manners [...] a body as absolute ».

To understand what happened during these more than 30 years of silence on the matter of the body inside Non-Philosophy, we have to give a glance in-depth inside Laruelle's theoretical evolution during the genesis of his non-equivalent matrix of thought.

Actually, it may occur to be easier to explain in a highly plausible way why the body has disappeared, rather than to tell why it comes back nowadays in Laruelle's itinerary.

When looking inside his unpublished Thesis[73], what appears at first about his approach of Heidegger's thinking thought is that, trying to see through our *hermeneutic libido*[74], body is deeply implied as a crucial concept in Laruelle's writing.

Laruelle acknowledges that Heidegger was the one « who has discovered the body of Being as a location or a site (*Ort*) though

[73] François Laruelle, *Économie des effets d'être* [*Economy of the effects-of-Being*], 2 Vol. (unpublished, Paris-Université de Nanterre, 1974.
[74] *Ibid.*, vol. 1, p. 23.

from a still Copernican mode of gathering :
World »[75]. But that World sounds already
pretty much Deleuzian :

> « Everywhere transcendental desire
> drills and fissures, produces syntheses
> which are short-circuits, circuit breakers
> but which relaunch a bit further,
> elsewhere and aside, supplements of
> disorganizing energy. And thereupon,
> elsewhere and always the closest to the
> inaudible voice of Being, its scarcely
> musical phonatoring machines, the
> cut-cutting hearing of some thinkers in a
> cluster, on *Topos*. It is at work every-
> where with processes, and processes
> function with effects ; each time the
> transcendental *Topos* reproduces on it,
> everywhere on it, the « small » local
> synthesis of sovereignty and the high
> synthesis of consumption [*consumation*,
> smouldering, squandering, in the sense
> that Georges Bataille (1897-1962) gave
> to it (TN)], whereas on one edge the
> process re-cleaves some signifieds, some
> terms, some instances, and on the other
> edge – though it's the same but with
> one difference – subject melts with
> jouissance, dissolves at consuming pro-
> ducts, without being required to orga-
> nize and relaunch the process, which
> undertakes producing « elsewhere » its

[75] *Ibid.*, p. 21.

effects, its segments and its reference – traveller without luggage who doesn't even have any path to let Thought go, and whose every trail absconds. Them, they do really go nowhere since they go astray in the desert of *Topos*, on the immense body of Being. »[76]

We could start thinking that, at this very point of emerging in Philosophy, the Body stands, according to Laruelle's position, as the non-Copernican name, the non-Galilean depiction, the non-Newtonian concept of Being as a place, as a *Topos*, as the anchoring field of being-there (*Da-sein*).

Behind this displacement, what Laruelle's gathers, melts, intimately merges, are Derrida's writing and Deleuze's multiple intensities (*i.e.* Klossowkian crests of *Stimmung*[77]).

---

[76] *Ibid.*, 15-16.

[77] Pierre Klossowski, *Nietzsche and the Vicious Circle*, trans. D. W. Smith (Chicago : University of Chicago Press, 1997) is a major reading to be done in order to catch Thought from this period. Although very discrete, **Pierre Klossowski** (1905-2001), as a high level translator, and even more as an essayist, is at least, himself also being a close friend of **Georges Bataille** (1897-1962), to be considered of the same influence as **Maurice Blanchot** (1907-2003) for xx[th] Century French thought.

Or was it ever already there, ever already done from the origin, « betrayal of origins being more originating than origin »[78], Laruelle

[78] François Laruelle, *op. cit.*, p. 23 ; *treason, Betrayal* (as

only making the struggle against Metaphysics more precise, more efficient, more incisive ?...

In fact, Laruelle is even more positive-affirmative than that : inside Writing and Deconstruction, « effects-of-Being function in a superb oblivion of Metaphysics »[79].

Hermeneutic libido, which animates the thinking Thought as a process of authentification, of singular/own/proper-Becoming (*Ereignis*)[80] – and which is through and through transcendental –, drives Being into exceeding itself, activating the liquidation of metaphysical syntheses (*Logos*, *Physis*, *Aletheia*, *Cogito*, Self-Consciousness, Spirit, Will...), but truly without needing to forget them, always under and beyond them – which are only repressive stoppings of Desire in representations, in constituted transcendences : effects-of-Being, as interpretative productions, affirming themselves inside Sense as transcendental dispersive singularities, as signifying differences :

« double turning-away ») having to be understood as one central Deleuzian concept, at least explicitly since 1977 : see the second part, « On the superiority of Anglo-American literature », in Gilles Deleuze & Claire Parnet, *Dialogues*, trans. H. Tomlinson & B. Habberjam (London : Athlone, 1987).
[79] François Laruelle, *op. cit.*, vol. 1, p. 21.
[80] *Ibid.*, p. 16.

« If there is a language of Being, it shall be the unclosed ensemble of effects-of-Being or differantial signs of Being functioning under random as disreason of their series. Not transcendent, even transcendental, signifieds or signifiers : transcendental dispersion excludes such modes of synthesis which are not rigourously constituter or producers of what they synthesize. All these conditions are fulfilled with hermeneutic energy, libido of interpretation, since it produces a fragmentation, but positive, of the body of Being into partial and full parts, into effects-of-Being, dualizing, dividing ; all this without interiority, for it is an immanent division, and for transcendental immanence is the outside ensemble of integrally positive outsides ; it distinguishes itself absolutely from interiority. »[81]

This positivity that Laruelle seeks to surpass **Martin Heidegger** with, is the positivity of putting desire and a transcendental sense inside the *Wesen des Seins* up to *the process of an intensive epoché freed from angst.*

[81] *Ibid.*, p. 21.

This urge for affirmative-active positivity runs through the all Philosophy 1 as a precise Nietzschean criterium of rigor to supplant any negative-reactive interpretations which imbue Metaphysics as such under the many appearances of conceptual cloaks :

> « All those compromises, those mixte beings, and even that nothinging which disguises a negation that has become shameful and that tries to conceive itself as nothinging of and inside Being, without reaching the differantial positivity of Being, they only express some travesties and repressing markings of intentional processes and of their positive cuttings, of derivations and normalizations of interpretations fluxes forming the specific acting of the

> essence-of-Being. As many organic limbos inside the non-organic body of Being ; as many representative hindrances on the transcendental Topos ; as many residues of negation within the functioning of desire. »[82]

Not only do we have to get that the One which Laruelle has discerned and has come to define in a radical new way comes directly from this matter, especially from the problematic of recurrence confronted with the Lévinassian problematic of the Finitude of Being and its im?potency[83]; but also we have

---

[82] *Ibid.*, p. 60.

[83] *How to conceive a theoretical matrix that embodies its own finitude (*i.e. *its decline) inside the laws of its machinic functioning* is one of the strongest and most rigorous demands that Laruelle confronts in Philosophy 1. When he amazingly deeply paid his tribute to **Emmanuel Lévinas** (1905-1995) by bringing together some of the most impactful writers of the former generation in a collective book (François Laruelle (ed.), *Textes pour Emmanuel Lévinas* (Paris : Jean-Michel Place, 1980), he was on the verge of giving his first formulation of what would lead him to break with both Deconstruction and Libidinal Machinism. He went to write about what he was calling at this very moment « the One-for-the-Other » :

> « Wouldn't it be in one respect the Earth itself, the only one Earth for the Other, the Subject as a hunting and flying ground for the

above all to grasp that this use, in his writing and in his conceptual weapons, of the semantic field of body is absolutely not a mere metaphor but it envelops the intimate and ultimate goals of his program for *making of the thinking thought a permanent treatment of onto-analysis*[84]:

> « Making eye and hearing think as differential noemata of the body of Topos as become inorganic, and affirming intentions of saliva and urine, of chyle and blood as « modes » of Thought, here is the assignment of the

Other, ground of war and peace intertwined, entangled, always side by side and never separated by the distance of an humiliation, of an inhibition, of a lateness ? Could the Beyond of essence, its exteriority, its invisibility have to suffer from this return not of the Same, but from the Return *as One* and from the One as full/plane body-of-the-Other ? » (*Ibid.*, p. 122).

[84] *Économie des effets d'être, op. cit.*, vol. 1, p. 30.

thought which isn't metaphysical anymore, which is not definable in Metaphysics : becoming the thinkers of an un-own body, O Phenomenologists of own body, of bodies-thinkers, of thinking-bodies. »[85]

Until the very last book from Philosophy 1, *Beyond the power principle*[86] – which is somehow, as much as it is certainly the most Lacanian book of Laruelle, the very attempt of an affirmative Deconstruction of Power, even already beyond Foucault from the very first lines of the introduction[87] –, Laruelle keeps exploring hermeneutics and political fields of production (both production of/from Sovereignty and Im?potency) through a conceptual set involving bodies :

« The two bodies invested of matter [empowered by matter, caught up by matter (TN)], the empirical one and the transcendental one, form a loop which, at its intersection, knots the minority subject. These are two mismatched

---

[85] *Ibid.*, p. 65.

[86] François Laruelle, *Au-delà du Principe de pouvoir* (Paris : Payot, 1978).

[87] A translation of this introduction, by T. Adkins, is available at : https://fractalontology.wordpress.com/ 2007/10/09/translation-francois-laruelles-preface-to-beyond-the-principle-of-power/

halves of History, one half with global and totalizing function, one half that carries out the power of subversive *Spaltung* and re-cleaves itself *continuously* = the resisting-revolutionary quarter = the object (r). »[88]

Ultimately Laruelle formulates the conceptual core of the political issue he aims to break through :

> « The problem that the minority faces and for which it must invent the daily solution – it would be wrong to believe it to be abstract and "philosophical" as stupidity says – is : how can I make myself a full/plane Body, a minor generality, how can I extirpate from Being, that is to say from my body, any foundation, soil or ground, any foundation and property ? It is only when the process of propriation (*Er-eignis*) (or of Determination) of generalities becomes a process of radical production of the subject, when the Er-eignis includes an Ent?eignis (a positive repression of the proper), that it becomes possible to say that, for the subject, his "being" as object (r) is at stake in his being ("is at stake in" : the process of (co)-propriation, the syntax of the minority). »[89]

[88] *Ibid.*, p. 56.
[89] *Ibid.*, p. 89.

And by convoking « fractional organs of power » that produce Power as it becomes a Body, especially a Body with a dominant regime (without the supposed might of any subject or any class, as Marxism as well as Bourgeoisie practice), Laruelle achieves here what he has begun to theorize as a truly embodied definition of Unilaterality from a pure Nietzschean approach of politics :

> « The machinic definition of Power goes through the complicity of the naturalist/technical versions of unconscious. Since the partial agent of Power *does not distinguish itself from its effects which distinguish themselves from it*, Thought is compelled to think this partial agent in the form of *a flux or of an instinctual fluancy which does not distinguish itself from the body that emits it…* »[90]

[90] François Laruelle, *Nietzsche contre Heidegger* (Paris : Payot, 1977), p. 111. The underlining is not from Laruelle's hand ; it focuses on the propositions that resituate Laruelle's strict formula of Unilaterality (*i.e.* the syntaxis of minorities) during his machinic developments : *x distinguishes itself from y which does not distinguish itself from it*. As we have seen above, Husserl has previously encountered this unilateral set when he was dealing with the problem of continuity, identifying singularities as different to others and simultaneously connected to the wholes.

Then, we can try and put forwards few hypotheses to understand the sudden occultation of the circumstances and contents of Flesh, of body, of any carnal aspects inside Laruelle's theory from 80's.

First of all, the turn which Laruelle operates in 1981, with the publishing of *The Minority Principle*[91], stands as the attempt to « define parts before whole and independently

[91] François Laruelle, *Le Principe de minorité* (Paris: Aubier Montaigne, 1981). The foreword of this book has been translated by E. Kazarian (2013) at : http://darkprecursor.net/2013/09/01/francois-laurelle-le-principe-de-minorite-foreword-in-english/ and a large extract, translated as « The Decline of Materialism in the Name of Matter, » is available in F. Laruelle, G. Alkon and B. Gunjevic, eds., *The Non-Philosophy Project* (New York : Telos Press, 2012), pp. 159-69.

of whole », to promote minorities « independently of any universal », *i.e.* the attempt to
define « immediate data of multiplicities »[92] as
being dispersive ones rather than continuous
ones – an attempt that can be understood as
the exact opposite of *Gestalt* theory[93] – and
which definitively bonds Laruelle rather with
Democritean Atomism[94].

By doing so, rather than putting forward,
Deleuzianly, a body-without-organs which un-
divisibly encompasses a machinic apparatus of
histological functions and syntaxes – as an
ultimate syntax of emptiness, as an utmost

[92] *Ibid.*, 5.

[93] Laruelle might have been specifically aware of
these questions around *Gestalt* as having been the
publisher in 1989 of Simondon's book in the series
which he was director of (Gilbert Simondon, *L'Individuation psychique et collective* (Paris : Aubier, 1989)).

[94] Such a statement is often misunderstood by readers
of the quantum non-standard 5th period of Laruelle's
theoretical deployment, because they seem to
assimilate Democritean atomism with Rutherford's
ante-quantic model.

Yet Democritus brings an extraordinary answer to
Zenon's Parmenidean paradoxes between material
space-time continuities and infinite ideal division
(while Rutherford provides a model to explain the
experiments that don't fit with Thomson's plum
pudding former model).

With that in mind, the non-philosophical concept
of *Cloning* might be considered as Laruelle's specific
answer to the hard problem of *Clinamen*…

function of exteriority and desertion –, Laruelle's approach implies forbidding any kind of body to be a whole assembling the disseminated organs, cutting being prior, former, than any form that could encompass matter, a matter of given dispersive identities.

As such, this rupture in Laruelle's first works, the one rupture which opens the way for Non-Philosophy to the formulating of its axiomatic method, is above anything else a rigorous and highly demanding reconsideration of the transcendental method, by redefining the transcendental cutting and the requirements of reduction as responding to the Principle of unilaterality that is applied as a ground rule :

« the residue extracted by the cutting, namely what we call the *a priori*, is identical

to cutting itself; the reduction is transcendental if it is the work of the residue in
person. Transcendental means immanent,
and the transcendental method isn't –
shouldn't be – the work of a Philosopher *ex
machina*. Because it is the work of the only
residual side, even identical to it, the cutting
is said uni-lateral. And, as the residue cuts
inside empirical continuities from which it
detached, the *a priori* is always both at once
what precedes experience and what deter-
mines it as a condition. »[95]

A complete Section of the book, « Of the
technology of Thought », is consecrated to
delineate this (« Beyond the Idea in general,
the dispersive », and « against transcendental
Idealism, transcendental matter »[96]), and it
culminates with one fundamental statement :
the real is cutting, and the cutting is subject[97].

It is easy to grasp that one obvious consequence of such a position is the eviction of
any empirical waste inside the methodological
matrix. And the Body, as a concept, can carry
far more empirical remnants than pure matter
can, especially matter as a pure dispersive field
of singular beings without any Idea to gather
them under its realm (like Being, *Hylé*,
Logos…).

[95] *Le Principe de minorité, op.cit.*, p. 39.
[96] *Ibid.*, p. 49.
[97] *Ibid.*, p. 56.

In the detail, we can find in Laruelle's thought one last sporadic attempt to adjudicate on the theoritical function that could occupy the Body, and how it could satisfy the non-philosophical requirements. At the turn of his Philosophy III, in his *Théorie des étrangers* (1995), Laruelle gives, in few paragraphs, a synthesis of the reasons why he distrusts the Body as a philosophically inherited concept, and how it has to be transformed to fit the theoretical demands of immanence. The extensive quoting that follows deploys the whole conceptual intrication inside which Philosophy maintains its stranglehold on/*via* the Body of man, as it shortly but definitively gives to the Body its limited quota :

> « That which we are also going to call the body of man will therefore no longer be an otherwise idealized physiological, anatomical, social, economical entity, etc. ; nor will it be a regional entity and utterly identifiable on the basis of empirical data. But it will be a universal aprioritico-transcendental structure, a supra-regional structure, independent of any empirical data, even if they were natural and biological, yet whose knowledge will depend on these data according to a relation that is defined as « occasional ».
>
> Therefore, we must change hypothesis : instead of thinking the body from itself, through the auto-position of empirical data,

attributing to it a refolding upon itself and a sufficiency – a Principle of Sufficient Body – which reestablishes philosophy in its rights, we will infer the body (as the Stranger) from the real cause, from the human-Ego-of-the-last-instance, even if this means to determine it afterwards in accordance with its knowledge. It is the only means to tear the « totality » of the human from the soul/body metaphysical hierarchy, which Phenomenology (Husserl, Merleau-Ponty, Heidegger) was not able to really forgot, like a poisoned hereditament, and which we know being fliped and inverted at will from Descartes to Nietzsche. And it is the only means to re-establish human within the Ego which gives its radical subjectivity to this body (of) the Stranger, an « objective » body, that is itself withal not an object.

Therefore, it is through the body – may it be understood in that sense as transcendental, but not ontological, as determined-in-the-last-instance by the Ego – that we exist completely as Stranger. If universal, non-political democracy (in the sense that we understand this « non ») wants to be a human democracy throughout rather than a supplementary abstraction or a political generality, *i.e.* one of the universals of « political science », it must be able to provide an absolutely subjective concept – though in-the-last-instance only – of the

Stranger or of its body ; and especially to reconcile at first these two determinations by tearing one from biology, the other from politics or history. The within-Ego-identity of the body and of the being-Stranger is only paradoxical for the philosophical distributions of reality, but it is understood from the point of view of a universal science of humans, which we see that it completly exceeds, through its scientific-type generality, the famous Nietzschean « disciplines » and the production of the modern body by the machines of micro-politics. These remain stuck within the apportionment of domination and Authority, in this spirit of hierarchy that philosophy will have not spared man.[98] »

[98] François Laruelle, *Théorie des Étrangers, Science des hommes, démocratie, non-psychanalyse,* Paris : Kimé, 1995 p.156-157 (draft translation with the help of Jeremy Ross Smith).

The second explanation of this conceptual and thematic disappearance of embodiment may be more empirical, very far from theoretical contents, and may fall within the ambit of psychology.

As noticed, Laruelle doesn't make much references and almost never makes quotes in his writings. The opening of his PhD dissertation, as quoted above in the foreword, gave the precisions that we commented on, in a twelve lines warning, about this stylistic and methodological decision he made very upstream to his work.

Rather than commenting on excerpts and passages, what Laruelle explains is that he has learnt uses of gestures. He has incorporated manners of thought, movements of conceptual writing, processes of demonstrations, of researches, of intellecting, which he has geared up to proceed by himself, towards his own goals and requirements.

Laruelle doesn't comment on other authors in the way one would study objects ; they are not. Why and How, since he analyses their process of thinking ?

The answer to these questions has taken a precise shape inside (and as) the immanentist protocol of Philosophy 1 :

What Laruelle aims to form is what he calls a *Problematic*:

> « this term denotes a precise func-tioning : the circle or the chiasma of reciprocal affection of Thought by its object, of the object by thought »[99],

> that is : organizing « the fusion in the last instance of the Libido and its theory »[100].

Laruelle lets his thought being imbued, animated and transformed by the works and the authors which he takes a close look at.

By analysing them, he acts them, he prolongs them, he makes new uses of their

---

[99] François Laruelle, *Le Déclin de l'écriture* (the Decline of Writing) (Paris : Aubier-Flammarion, 1977), p. 8.
[100] *Ibid.*, 21.

tools, he uses by himself their tools on each other, he makes of his own thought a machine composed with parts, energies, functions… taken and assembled from theirs.

In such an extent that we sometimes happen to ask, while reading his PhD dissertation, whether it is a pastiche or an intimate living legacy, and how we can decide in his lines between utmost seriousness and ludic musical frenzy of thought.

As he was explaining with very rare details the birth of Non-Philosophy, in a preface for the first book ever written on his work[101], Laruelle indicated the extreme point of circumstances that had been the substitution

---

[101] Juan Diego Blanco, *Initiation à la pensée de F. Laruelle* (Paris : L'Harmattan, 1997). This preface, entitled « What is Non-Philosophy ? » has been translated by T. Adkins and published in François Laruelle, *From Decision to Heresy* (Falmouth : Urbanomic/New York : Sequence, 2012), pp. 185-244.

operated by Michel Henry, the change of transcendental field towards a new ontological episteme that the latter had accomplished, in silence, unheralded and unseen for a long time after by academics and post-Heideggerian philosophers : the rising from the deepest philosophical oblivion of Ipseity, of Identity, of what Laruelle would call the One.

Knowing how far, how essentially Henry has correlated this unexampled, un-mundane, un-monist (ontologically speaking) immanence with Flesh, Arche-Body, Incarnation, we could assume that, just escaped from Deleuze's influence and conceptual apparatus, the rigorous requirements of invention, of thought, of sovereignty also, may have brought Laruelle to avoiding to pour himself into another inherited set of concepts, into another pattern of syntax ; to avoid falling from one body(-without-organs) to an (auto-affective) other.

What he was thirsting for, was another use of the One.

It was not to jump from one philosophy to another, neither to get out of Philosophy, but to get rid of its resistance, especially its resistance to be once each time invented anew by being reduced to a mere occasional material.

So Laruelle had to cut his own path, he had to excise his own course of invention, if he wanted to bring anything new to Thought, a new method, a new syntax, a new set of concepts : new usages to be shared and improved collectively.

As we have told in detail on the recent occasion of a celebratory context[102], the collectives of researchers, of thinkers, of students or artists who have neighboured Laruelle as fellow inventers or who have gathered around him, and have supported Non-Philosophy and participated in its development (during its early emergence in reviews like *La Décision Philosophique*, or while it was gaining international influence, especially with the creation of *ONPhI* – the Interna-

[102] See « Giving an Identity : Coordinates of Invention. Heresy and Dissidence Among Non-Philosophers », in *Identities : Journal for Politics, Gender and Culture*, 2018, *15*(1-2), pp. 118-156. https://doi.org/10.51151/identities.v15i1-2.341

tional Non-Philosophic Organization), have brought occasions to confront Laruelle again with embodiment, affects, flesh, pathemes, and thus to reveal deeper implications of his remoteness from body.

With the 1998 intervention of **Gilles Grelet** (1971-), and the proposition of Gnosis which the latter has put forth by delineating the unexpected field of Non-Religion[103], Laruelle had clearly to take a stance, and he did in 2004 by writing *Struggle and Utopia at the End Times of Philosophy* as an answer to Grelet's breakthroughs, because the political attitude, the theoretical orientation and the directions to be followed by the

[103] See Gilles Grelet, « un Bréviaire de Non-Religion, » in François Laruelle (ed.), *Discipline Hérétique* (Paris: Kimé, 1998) – the Preface has been translated in François Laruelle, *From Decision to Heresy op. cit.*, pp. 257–284 ; Gilles Grelet, *Déclarer la Gnose – d'une Guerre qui revient à la culture* [*Declaring Gnosis – about a war that gets back to Culture*] (Paris : L'Harmattan, 2002) ; Gilles Grelet, « Anti-Phénoménologie », in *Revue philosophique de la France et de l'étranger* 129, no. 2 (2004), pp. 211-24 ; Gilles Grelet, « Gnose Prolétarienne, » *#TRANSISTOR*, DVD-ROM (FR-Plancy-L'Abbaye : INgens, 2012), available as « Proletarian Gnosis, » *Angelaki : Journal of Theoretical Humanities* Vol. 19, Nr 2 (April 2014), pp. 93-98 and the recent Gilles Grelet, *Theory of the Solitary Sailor* (UK-Falmouth : Urbanomic, 2022)

members of ONPhI were at stake in the relation that they both had developed with each other.

https://www.dailymotion.com/video/xzfsg

Grelet's Gnosis, personified and concretely actualized into the figureheads of the *Rebel* and the *Angel* (as non-religious forms of the subject), was driven under the specific condition of manic-depression, Enthusiasm and Melancholy alternating in an immediate reciprocation of human greatness with naked horror[104].

This entrenchment in pathos, in affects, considered to be Thought as well as Rationalities are, was depicted to be the ground of the Gnostic Rebellion's double irrationalist, theosophical and messianic imperative : *not to believe in death* and *play the Angel*[105]:

---

[104] Gilles Grelet, *Déclarer la Gnose, op. cit.*, p. 96.
[105] *Ibid.*, p. 95.

« From there, a major consequence which is formulated : *between rationality and irrationality passes the split line of the sufficiency to the thought of the propositional structure*; the real of rationality integrally boiling down to its enunciation and to the propositions which impose from it, as contrary to the real of irrationality, for which thought inscribes itself inside a structure that thought exceeds in every way. »[106]

Facing this unpredicted line inside non-philosophical theory – a line that divinises Division in the name of a real which is war itself[107], a war against this enemy that is the agnostic rationality because the latter deploys death as a necessity[108] – Laruelle chose to identify the instance of the Angel as a repeat of Platonic *mania*[109], and opposed to « Saint Gilles » that beginning « with a religious reduction of philosophy », « emasculating philosophy as imaginary makes the task easier »[110]: such « deficient analyses or limits of

[106] *Ibid.*, pp. 11-12.
[107] *Ibid.*, p. 66.
[108] *Ibid.*, p.. 80.
[109] François Laruelle, *Struggle and utopia at the End Times of Philosophy*, trans. D. S. Burk and A. P. Smith (2004 ; Minneapolis : Univocal, 2012), p. 220.
[110] *Ibid.*, p. 149; « Imaginary » refers to the Lacanian concepts (R,S,I) which Grelet adopts in his theorization.

philosophy » only leading to Philosophy's « return in the form of the sufficiency of a theological or philosophical « absolute » »[111].

But, what is more deeply important, Laruelle underlined – because of Religion inside Grelet's theorism being « more world-thought than Philosophy » – that « it does not provide either the adequate vocabulary nor the critical technique that philosophy provides and which are necessary in order to be able to speak of non-religion in the name of the Real. »[112]

This position of Laruelle is of great importance regarding to the Body and em- bodied experience because it definitively forbids Non-Philosophy to take ever any theoretical account of contents that have not been previously treated by Philosophy itself, by Rationality and its critical procedures, its lexicon and its logical syntaxes, *i.e.* that have not been previously conceptualized or referred to concepts in some way.

That is to say that there may not be, inside Laruelle's Non-Philosophy, any Vision-in-One for carnal experience, that there may not be any experience outside *Logos* to be lived according-to-the-One, to be explored, descri-

[111] *Ibid.*, 178-79.
[112] *Ibid.*, 187.

bed and spoken « in the name of the Real », neither affects, feelings, emotional condition (*mania*) nor body states, cœnæsthesia, motor functions, hormonal levels or autonomic nervous system activities...

For instance, **Francisco Varela**'s (1946-2001) experiments on *The Embodied Mind* at the Mind & Life Institute, based on meditation and contemplative traditions, which have led Richard J. Davidson (1951-) to breakthroughs in immunology[113], wouldn't take any place inside the contemplative device of Non-Philosophy.

Here may lie Laruelle's own « unaware » decision.

A decision that drives Non-Philosophy from its very beginning as a residue of its post-Structuralist origins.

By founding the non-philosophical project of generalizing Deconstruction, Laruelle seems to having been dragged into enlarging Derrida's Deconstructive reduction, the reduction of Consciousness to Text and of concepts to metaphors ; but by doing so his

---

[113] Richard J. Davidson, « Alterations in Brain and Immune Function Produced by Mindfulness Meditation, » *Psychosomatic Medicine* 65 (2003): pp. 564–570.

enlargement happened to be the enlargement of the reduction of every phenomenon to Philosophy.

Even in the case of Grelet's Non-Religion, Laruelle needed the material to be first reduced by/to Philosophy before being admissible inside Non-Philosophy.

We can assume that non-philosophical apparatus finds here its limits : it only operates on rationalized materials, on conceptualized matrices of discourse, on a World that has already ever been reduced to Philosophy.

Hence its reluctance to face and consider irrationality, *mania*, psychopathology or affects, pathemes, prenoetic sensitivity, *i.e.* antepredicative situations, as being legitimate in its field of creativity and analysis.

This may be related to Laruelle's own path through Heideggerian Hermeneutics and through Structuralism : he has inherited *Logos*-centred tools and Saussurian conceptions of Representation and Meaning.

Moreover it may be as well related to Laruelle's old-established generalization of political concerns and deeply rooted diffidence vis-à-vis theology[114].

But what if Thought hasn't been beforehand likened to *Logos* but could be enlarged to non-conceptual or non-conceptualized experiences (like are affects, impressions, motor reflexes, visceral behaviours…), enlarged to experiences which haven't been formerly placed under the mastery of rationality and which may be not merely solvable into philosophical discourse – but yet have a legitimate place in a true contemplative set, from the Vision-in-One and in the name of the real, at first as embodied immediate experiences or, maybe more accurately, as unconceptualized events happening to a sensitive formless lived matter ?

---

[114] At least from *Nietzsche contre Heidegger* (1977), and its libidinal-political cutting, to *Introduction to Non-Marxism*, trans. A. P. Smith (2000 ; Minneapolis : Univocal Publishing, 2015).

Ten years before Grelet happened to Non-Philosophy, Laruelle had already once been confronted with such a question from one of his early intimate friends and fellow thinkers, **Serge Valdinoci** (1947-).

Not much of the latter's theoretical work has been translated into English for now, but some is[115].

What Valdinoci has put forth was an immanentist theory of invention, rather rooted in Psychiatry and Psychopathology than in Structuralism and litterature, rather entrenched inside affects and cœnæsthesia, proprioception and pathemes, than connected to *Logos*, concepts or representations.

[115] One can consult the remaining translation of the opening of *Towards a Method of europanalysis* (1995), by Jesse Newberg, at : http://ingens.eu/index.php/pages/73-europanalysis-english-version or https://web.archive.org/web/20130422180523/http://cups.zxq.net/

In 2013 Valdinoci gave an abstract on his method of thought, a method called *europanalysis* :

What is to be contemporary with *Poïein* ?

Poetry, from Greek *poïesis* (ποίησις), noun, " Creation, fabrication " & *poïein* (ποιεῖν), verb, " To make, to produce, to create ".

Entrance

The World-Men almost always have Reasons to be right. When they think, they reproduce a Picture-book Absolute that withdraws them from Thought. That is why it is necessary to break through, to pass the cultural bridge by which the World proceeds. The Picture-book Absolute must carry itself away to a **sublogic** that must not fear to **associate** in order to figure out, in the potencyful affect, the **viscera-pathemes** that scroll over the silent affect. Up to us, on the borders of this Reason-Thought, to experience the sublogic, to integralize the viscering within this visceral.

Notation

"True Thought", which encountered only very rarely, is invention as ***poïesis***. Invention is continual, must struggle against the narrow, even violent, moments of the psycho-intellectual apparatus. Essentially poïetic, Thought, at last far from its substance, is *transubstantiation*. The searched invention plunges into the immensity of the ploughing chaos. A sublogic have to avoid putting in superficial plans, redoing *basis* of its *metabasis*-as-ink-of-abyss. Thus characterized in this way, Thought is intrinsically inventive, æsthesiologically. The contemporary is not always a slice of life examinable from a knowledge. The fundamental *poïesis*, which is without spatiotemporal determinations, is above all the chaotic gaping of a fundamental ***khôra***, duly reactivated (Plato, *Timæus*).

Connotation

Returned to gaping, to the in-hollow of foundations, a prescience works, but no longer within metaphors that reconvoke a Picture-book regime. On the contrary, a non-fetishized instance loads the variation positively *via* the connotative work of the in-

internal inscription. This increase of load quarters the spirit, as it is invaded from inside by a ***mysterium tremendum*** that clamors for a clinic of the symptoms that connote the black great mystery.

Denotation

In the contemporary of any ***poïein***, whatever the dimensions of the local ***theorein***, ***immensity*** prevails, without *dimensional*, while a general clinic replaces the restricted cultural clinic of the medical art. Thus extended, it becomes civilizational ; it treats of recollection inside recollection in internal. It mystically fades to multiply the in-hollows in a Pathetics of Universe.

Envoy

To this extent only, the moments of a sublogic **in-invention** get distinguished. The reader will see there an attempt of self-elucidation. This is because one's own reader's thought, at first engaged, there gradually disentangles. »[116]

---

[116] Serge Valdinoci, « Qu'Est-Ce Qu'Être Contemporain Du *Poïein* ? » *Dézopilant*, n° 19 (September 2014).

Grown up side by side with Laruelle's Non-Philosophy during the early 80's[117], this visceral mystics settles immediately : before any distance neither any synthesis, inside Flesh, inside visceral lived – but lived, experienced, as a moving cœnæsthetic embedding of philosophical (= European) representations, inside a primal inner collapse, which Valdinoci names, rather than the One : *Endon*, the Internal[118].

Laruelle and Valdinoci are both about a primal dispersive cutting, about a « normal state of *epoché* »[119].

But for Valdinoci this « phenomenon of positive loss of *Logos* for the benefit of the real »[120] is a full-blown experience, the « inalterable human experience of *Krisis* »[121].

[117] Valdinoci was very active within the first collective of non-philosophical interests. All the workers were gathering around the review *La Décision Philosophique*.
[118] The psychiatric concept of *Endon* is specifically developed by Hubertus Tellenbach, a major figure of the Phenomenological Psychiatry who worked on *Atmosphere*, and who has approached this notion of *Endon* when inquiring into *Melancholy : History of the Problem, Endogeneity, Typology, Pathogenesis, Clinical Considerations, Volume 9*, trans. E. Eng (1974 ; Pittsburgh : Duquesne University Press, 1980) – see p. 156.
[119] Serge Valdinoci, *Introduction dans l'europanalyse* (Paris : Aubier, 1990), p. 40.
[120] *Ibid.*, p. 20.
[121] *Ibid.*, p. 30.

And this ordinary state of crisis is to be considered as being Thought as such (and as being detailed, studied, explored, deployed as such ; here is the goal of europanalysis) ; for Laruelle it is not.

This reaches even a deeper level when *crisis* etymologically appears to be *decision* per se…

That's why Laruelle and Valdinoci's collaboration didn't survive Laruelle's 1995 turn to Philosophy 3.

Introducing *Cloning* (instead of the complex syntaxis of the (Non)-One elaborated in *Biography of Ordinary Man*[122]), and introducing occasional (philosophical) transcendence as a necessary material, the publication of Laruelle's *Principles of Non-Philosophy*[123] has above all been the occasion to formulate the definitive foreclosure of the One for any exposition, *i.e.* the positing of a fundamental limit for the non-philosophical project.

The building of a taboo, according to Valdinoci's point of view.

---

[122] François Laruelle, A *Biography of ordinary man : On Authorities and Minorities*, trans. J. Hock (Hoboken : Wiley, 2018).

[123] François Laruelle, *Principles of Non-Philosophy*, trans. N. Rubczak & A. P. Smith (1996 ; London : Bloomsbury, 2013).

But this limit was first and foremost a limit to *Logos*, to concepts or to Representations, and, let's say also, a limit to the hermeneutical power, to the interpretative compulsion, of Metaphysics and Ontology, *i.e.* of Mastery[124].

It was a limit for any linguistic pretention to be ever able to tell the real in any way…

Unless you treat language otherwise than Ontology does ; unless you quit being worried about how representations could (or could not) expose the real, and envision for now on how the real *imposes* itself from itself to representations (which is one true consequence of Unilaterality[125]).

When the Structuralism succeeded to Existentialism, it did so like a space-thought would succeed to a Time-thought (inherited from Hegelianism and historical dialectics),

---

[124] *Beyond the Power principle* (*op. cit.*) was precisely this attempt to sketch a political hermeneutics that puts an end to « the power of meaning » in the name of minorities.

[125] Unilaterality which Valdinoci calls *precedence* (fr. *préséance*), to mark a conceptual distinction with Derrida's analyses of the metaphysics of *presence*, in the name of a deeper *general impression ;* see *Vers Une Méthode d'euro-panalyse* (Paris : L'Harmattan, 1995), pp. 123-26.

like a tabular ontology would succeed to a linear Ontology.

Looking for a radical transcendental lever, for a pure immanent spot of lived exteriority, unilaterally opposed to the realm of Representation, Laruelle has inadvertently maintained a classical use of language, a very traditional understanding of Semantics, and a very conventional division of Thought and Reality *via* the mainstream concept of Representation[126].

And doing so he could be himself exposed to his own reproach of « mak[ing] the task easier. »

On the contrary, admitting that escaping perception, and its phenomenological distances, implies exiting from the transcendental Kantian structure of both Time and Space that comes with, Valdinoci opted to accompany his theory of invention with a new set of considerations about language, axed by the concept of vivid (raw, searing) inscription.

Following the thinker whom he was maybe the closest to (at least among French authors),

---

[126] See for example his recourse to the distinction of noetic and noematic contents, in François Laruelle, *Philosophy and Non-Philosophy*, trans. T. Adkins (1989 ; Minneapolis : Univocal, 2013), pp. 62-73.

Maurice Merleau-Ponty[127] – the thinker of Flesh as « a generalized overflight inside absolute verticality »[128] –, Valdinoci assumes to restore Semantics to body, rather than to nurture a spiritualist opposition between understanding and matter anymore.

Indeed europanalysis considers Perception to be circular ; always mixing interiority-of-

[127] Serge Valdinoci, *Merleau-Ponty dans l'invisible*, (Paris : L'Harmattan, 2003); but Merleau-Ponty is a theoretical endorsement for Valdinoci since *Vers Une Méthode d'europanalyse*, especially concerning the development of the concepts of *Retro-reference* or *non-completion*, but above all of *Ultraperception* and *Endoception*.

[128] Serge Valdinoci, « Vers l'autre demarche : Ruyer, Merleau-Ponty, Deleuze, » in Louis Vax & Jean-Jacques Wunenburger, eds., *Raymond Ruyer. De la science à la théologie* (Paris : Kimé, 1995), 197-210. The concept of *absolute overflight* is here of major meaning. Raymond Ruyer promoted this crucial concept in order to indicate the experience that Deleuze called later the *Plan(e) of immanence*. Serge Valdinoci was one of Ruyer's Student before his PhD with Paul Ricœur. This path enlights pretty acurately why Valdinoci shares a different approach of Gnosis, monism and dualism than Laruelle's.

For more details about Ruyer non-dualistic Gnosis and his conception of body/consciousness, see « D'un corps à son image : Hans Jonas et le modèle rédempteur de la chair », in : *Revue Philosophique de Louvain* Vol. 117, issue 2, may 2019, pp. 341-374 : DOI: 10.2143/RPL.117.2.3287390

Idea and exteriority-of-object, it consists in a philosophical hallucinatory infinite (Hippolyte Taine) :a *proton pseudos*.

On the contrary, in the name of the black mystical Thought of invention, viscerally immanent, thoroughly blind, Valdinoci evokes a semantic sensibility (for example when one feels joy), prior to any differentiation of any object or any subject.

Valdinoci calls this inner dark matter of sense *generalized æsthesis*, *geometral* (Merleau-Ponty) or *ideopathy*, the latter meaning that, in Internal, pathos and meaning are one, and are felt upstream of constitution[129].

In that antepredicative frame of complete desidealized intuition, representations are ploughed, soaked with the terebration of the real.

[129] This upstream impression is described by Valdinoci under the movement of *Analectics* and is methodically set inside the praxis of *Geneanalysis* (generative analysis). But as a lived experience inside the radicality of reduction, it is explored within the terms of psychopathological experience : it takes place as an impressive *clinic* reversal or *in*version (examining a lying (re*clin*ed) patient), especially in the situation of the psychiatric clinical relation (the naked re*lying* on a caregiver to take in one's suffering) : « the pathological state is perhaps pure existence » (Serge Valdinoci, *Le Principe d'Existence* [The Existence Principle] (The Hague : Nijhoff, 1989), p. 1.

They rely on an inscription of immediacy at the very birth of knowledge (Merleau-Ponty's *co-naissance*, derived from **Paul Claudel** (1968-1955)), when the reciprocal affection of Thought by its object, of the object by Thought, is not fossilized by distances and intellectually reconquered through the still

spatial form of a chiasma – but genuinely felt as a primal chaotic *pathos*, an impressive *grounding collapse*, consisting in *interested, engaged, immersed representations*, rather than distanced, objectified, disinterested representations that language carries under the protocol of European ontologies of exteriority (the Greek luminous *Phaïnomenon* which Michel Henry has confronted inside Otological Monism) [130].

[130] Let's not forget, by the way, that Laruelle considers Merleau-Ponty's concept of chiasmus of no interest to be deepened and increased in the name of the Invisible, but to be one more avatar of the ideal englobing of Difference, or Being. On that, see

Within the infrastructure of this generalized æsthesis, what Valdinoci names *Endoception* involves vivid (raw) presentations of immediacy and im*mens*ity (as opposed to the ontological obsession with limits, measures, or di*mens*ions).

Moreover the phenomenological psychiatric concepts of ambiance, *Stimmung* or atmosphere – especially expounded by **Hubertus Tellenbach** (1914-1994) as well as he explored throughout melancholy the concept of *endon* (see note 115 above) – add an intersubjective depth that allows to bypass the hallucinatory infinite of otherness in the exact same way europanalysis demands to bypass the infinite of perceptive objects[131].

Philosophies of difference, trans. Rocco Gangle (London : Continuum, 2010) & « Du Monde comme méthode », in *Merleau-ponty, le psychique et le corporel*, ed.Anna-Theresa Tymieniecka (Paris : Aubier, 1988).

[131] See H. Tellenbach, (1981) « Tasting and smelling - taste and atmosphere – atmosphere and trust, » *Journal of Phenomenological Psychology*, Vol. 12, No. 2 (1981), pp. 221-30. Both Henry and Valdinoci have proposed to answer Husserl's Cartesian problem with the alter-ego rather from the inside than from the outside, which was Lévinas' solution (and, by extension, Derrida's) ; see « For a phenomenology of community, » in Michel Henry, *Material Phenomenology*, trans. S. Davidson (1990; New York : Fordham University Press, 2008). Giacomo Rizzolatti's 1996

objectivization and 2010 confirmation of mirror neurons (Rizzolatti & *Alii*, « Premotor cortex and the recognition of motor actions », *Cognitive Brain Research* 3 (1996), pp. 131-141 and Rizzolatti & Fabbri-Destro, « Mirror neurons: from discovery to autism », *Exp Brain Res.* 200, no. 3-4 (2010), pp. 223-37) has seemed to corroborate Husserl's option with empathy, and might add to the promises of Varela Neurophenomenological project ; but Henry rather follows the trails opened by hypnosis (demonstrating here interesting aspects of Unilaterality). Laruelle's matrix clearly avoids these questions around intersubjectivity by stating that the One stands in a Solitude precedent to even Solipsism (see « A Rigorous Science of Man, » in *A Biography of Ordinary Man, op. cit.* or *From Decision to Heresy, op. cit.,* pp. 33–73).

These are two manners to break consequently with transcendental space-time superstructure of perception and to escape the philosophical *partes extra partes* (a Latin expression used by Raymond Ruyer).

This incarnated sense and feeling of semantics, envisaged as an embodied inter-subjective immediate given, manifests itself through *tact*, which is both a sense of direct inner intimate touch (rather than *contact*, which is related to remaining distances) ; and a sensitive care to shared and mutually constructed bodily lived meanings in a prior situation where subjects aren't anymore real accepted limits.

The Other always emerges from a starting point of individualism, whether it is Cartesian as ego in Knowledge or Heideggerian as *Dasein* in chosen ones' angst.

Valdinoci opens to the stance of a prior infra-subjective, infra-individual, intersubjective or trans-subjective embodied semantics from whom he understands civilization, but only under the wider integral impression of the immense universe[132].

[132] Serge Valdinoci, « La Science de l'Homme immense, » in *La Décision Philosophique*, no. 9 (1989), pp. 65-79.

That is why his theory is presented as a europanalysis, rather than a Psychoanalysis (Freud, Jung, Ferenszi, Lacan), a *Daseinsanalysis* (Binswanger, Maldiney, Schotte) or even a Fate-analysis (Szondi). It is no longer a theoretical construction around limits, especially the limit of subjectivity, consciousness or individuation (which always carts the unsolvable problem of the articulation of the encounter, the syntaxes of contacts, the dialectics of opposed positions – with the object, the other, the collective, the World… a problem to which Laruelle's *Cloning* tries to answer). It is rather a practice of immensity through one's own continental participation (to) the real, through the methodical collapsing of cultural determinations by the self siderating void of one integralized *epoché*.

This immanentist principle of immersion, which is inherency (at least ipseity, but without any concerns in being unary anymore, unity having no more to do with an innerly lived chaos of invention), has to be related to Merleau-Ponty's lesson about *Gestalt* that Structuralists have omitted :

« there is structure only in situation. »[133]

[133] Maurice Merleau-Ponty, *Psychologie et pédagogie de l'enfant. Cours de Sorbonne 1949-1952* (FR-Lagrasse : Verdier, 2000), p. 275.

Valdinoci's *in-Intuition*, *in-Internal* or what he calls the hyperbolic structures of *in-hollows*, are the mystical translation of what Varela has locally brought further from connectionism and autopoïesis into embodiment and enactment : the deep-rooted *enclosure* (of) the real, rather than its foreclosure (which is always a foreclosure *to* something external, whether *Logos*, Transcendence or World-Philosophy, bumping on limits…).

Here, this use of foreclosure reveals the blatant fragility of Laruelle's non-philosophical building when addressing the question of the living body , and reveals the way Laruelle has vouched more and more for his Lacanian (*i.e.* Structuralist) legacy.

The manner with which he has avoided, both with Grelet in 2004 and with Valdinoci in 1996, to take full account of what they call *Pathemes*, these parts of experience that are natively extraneous to language but incarnate the proto-manifestation of meaning[134], is strikingly symptomatic on that matter.[135]

What we can notice is that Laruelle has progressively gone from an 80's initial proof-experienced description of the One as a lived affect of dispersive cutting inherency[136], to a purely symbolic use of the One inside theorematic-axiomatic matrices very much closer to *Mathemes*[137].

That's precisely what he had formerly already been tempted to do once in 1978 by calling it, in an obvious Lacanian way, the

[134] Remembering his former works on Husserl's *Ur-affektion* (the *Ur-hylé* of the living originating flux of prejacent passivity), Valdinoci explained in a 1997 conference that the europanalytic project was following the line of a *Phenomenopathy* rather than a Phenomenology (Serge Valdinoci, *L'Économie du sacrifice chez Georges Bataille* (FR-Reims : Le Clou dans le fer, 2004) : « what we could name a theory that is not a theory *on* or a theory *about*, but a theory which, from the beginning, is a theory *inside*, or an investive/engaged *theoria.* »

[135] See Narciso Aksayam, « Giving an identity… » *op.cit.*

[136] François Laruelle, *Philosophy and Non-Philosophy*, *op. cit.*, pp. 37-45.

[137] Lacan introduced this concept, taken from Claude Levi-Strauss' concept of *Mytheme*, in 1971 in order to name *the writing of what we do not talk about but which can be transmitted*, in an obviously anti-Wittgensteinian way.

object (r) : one resisting revolutionary residue, unable to be assimilated in the economy of Power (either of Politics and of Hermeneutics), that *essentially* fractionates powers, being the condition of invention of the political continent[138].

[138] Even in the case of Fascism, that fastens it « in one event, one history, one memory, one people, one given class » ; *Beyond the power principle, op. cit.*, pp. 51-61. Valdinoci rather approaches this field of Revolution/subversion/invention inside the emblematic of an internal *In*surrection (*Erhebung*) ; see Serge Valdinoci, « *Écriture et immanence* [writing and immanence], » in *Abrégé d'europanalyse. La pensée analytique et continentale* (Paris : L'Harmattan, 1999), pp. 52-84.

Probably the genetic historical form of the present paper is contra-structuralism in essence.

And maybe it is our turn to face the risk of « making the task easier » when following the way we do this historical path that brings to light unformulated theoretical decisions that have come with Structuralism, or French Theory, and then have infused Laruelle's Non-Philosophy when regarding the Body.

But linguistic structures, conceptual assemblages, axiomatic delineations, are — rather than being once more endlessly criticized — just to be known as they are : local intellectual propositions among multiplicities of others, which sometimes follow trails that opens new fields of experience and new stances of behaviour while at the very same moment lead to dead ends when digging other lodes.

We just have to assess their local power of revelation, their partial efficiency of mastery and/or emancipation, their determinate range of praxis or their fractional width of contemplation.

But above all, we have to move on – peculiarly when talking about Earth…

Because Earth – as have recalled both Mach with the gravity reference frame for the unity of our sensations, and Husserl with the *Lebenswelt* and the immobile Ark/Arche of significations for the constitution of our experience[139]–, because Earth is the lived material that organizes our intersubjective situation of actions, which is inextricably meaning and movement, agency and feedback, our own living Earth of sensorimotricity.

But as the becoming-structure of our understandings, including the layers of our theoretical constructions, not only do we have

---

[139] See Edmund Husserl, « Foundational Investigations of the Phenomenological Origin of the Spatiality of Nature : The Originary Ark, the Earth, does not move, » in Leonard Lawlor (Ed.), M. Merleau-Ponty & E. Husserl, *Husserl at the Limits of Phenomenology* (US-Evanston : Northwestern University Press, 2002), pp. 117-131.

to move on, to explore further our own growth among the labyrinth of embodied psyches that we share as an economy of interrelated streams ; but we also have constantly, once each time, to move in, to dwell in, to immerge and bathe each of our statements, each of our decisions, each of our gestures inside this immanent ecumene which penetrates us while we go through.

Maybe we do not have to take a side, we do not have to make the choice to follow or not to follow Laruelle or his forebears and predecessors.

This decision has been theirs ; at least, if they weren't aware of, it was their determination.

And our logocentric and Apollonian thoughts as well as our anthropological socialized objective bodies have learnt pretty much by practicing by their sides.

So maybe we can fudge this decision that leads to approach the World as if it were Hell, an infinitely distanced Hell for nobody to penetrate inside, a Hell for each One to essentially ever already escape from[140].

---

[140] Because we could – as well as considering the One not to be philosophical anymore when not to be climbed towards in order to be reached, but already

Maybe we can move on and enlarge, widen, deepen this experience of immanent reduction, dispersion, cutting, night acid, grounding collapse that we are intimately, which is our moving flesh (of) Internal, the flesh of these insiders that we are, inside limits themselves :

inhabitants of cuttings themselves.

given like immanence as such — consider that the World is already redeemed and has ever been Hell only from a philosophical decision point of view also.

As illustrated back there, the method of europanalysis has kept moving on. By being a method geared in fluence, by being the flood itself of invention as a method.

But also, in the present details of considerations, by abandoning the inherited theoretical use of language like an exuviæ indeep, like the continuous and multiple ecdysis of our organogeneses, which are part of the identitygeneses of our bodies.

Doing so Immanence has abandoned the xx[th] century of Thought, as being a late symptom of agitation, somehow in between philosophical bedlam, ontological upraor, intellectual rowdiness and jeargonish linguistic hullabaloo. And consequetly it has led Immanence to renounce the usual Darwinian humanoïd struggles around the saliences of Law and Power, relegating the narrowness of Politics for the benefit of mystics, in the universe's line of invention as pure matter of drives, as pure self-curving way of traverse of the vertiginous *Theoros* that we are.

As it is penetrated by an absolute silence within, Valdinoci's in-fluence on contemporary Thought has been discrete, althought europanalysis has already opened researches rooted in the requisites of embodiment and enclosure : in Psychoanalysis and lexicology, with **Didier Moulinier**[141] ; in Pedagogy, with **Gérard Kponsou** and his *Doxology*[142] ; in Martial Arts, with **Romain Hennequin** and

[141] Early Internet explorer, Didier Moulier's work is at the crossroad of lacanism, Non-Philosophy, europanalysis and he is one of the most important publisher of contemporean poetry since 80's : https://www.netvibes.com/didier-moulinier#Mes_livres   consulted on april 6th 2022

[142] Gérard Kponsou, *De La Doxologie*, (FR-Plancy-L'Abbaye : INgens, 2022) & « L'approche doxologique de la contractualité : essai d'élucidation phénoménologique du contrat social, » in *Les Cahiers de l'Actif* n° 396/397 (mai-juin 2009), pp. 171-84.

the Hyonmudo, in South Korea ; in Music, with **Corso Samara**, a.k.a. Christophe Samarsky[143] ; and even in Hypnosis, with

[143]Corso, *Chaologies*, Jamendo, last modified May 11, 2008 : https://www.jamendo.com/album/24749/chaologies and https://corso.bandcamp.com/

A. Peltier in Belgium.

But it is clearly inside the domain of Poetry, precisely because of its complete reconsideration of Language usages, that europanalysis has produced its most interesting and until now its most influent trend of investments and creations : from, distantly, the experimental œuvre of **Michaël Batalla**[144] to, closerly, the pictorial existential poetry of **Nicolas Rozier**[145] ; more intimately from the

[144] https://ohlesbeauxjours.fr/programme/les-invites/michael-batalla/
[145] https://www.nicolasrozier.fr/

Nocturnal readings of Contemporary Poetry staged by the INgens Brozherhood[146] to, facetiously, the profoundly humoristic asceticism of **Ali Lham**[147].

It seems that europanalysis has concentrated, focused, in its breakthrough, a deep historical stream of Poetics concerns with the living experience of Body, with Semantics and

[146] http://ingens.eu/index.php/nocturnes/64-nocturne-de-poesie-contemporaine

[147] Ali Lham, whose thought stands at the crossroad of Valdinoci's and Peter Sloterdjik's, whom he transformed into a Henri Michaux and a Franz Kafka nutured by Chaplin (he has also worked on translating Ken Wilber into French), has recently published, few years after the Manisfest of the *Mouvement Cr@ckaïste*, a long-winded interview about Non-Spirituality : « Pour un Non-Éveil Radical Furtif. Entretien avec Ali de Saint-Sens, » [Towards a radical subreptice Non-Awakening *Cercle Rationné des Artistes Cleptomanes*, last modified December 23, 2018 : http://crakosm.org/nerf-de-la-paix/

Emptiness ; a stream that goes at least from the Mallarmean sideration experience of nothingness, *via* Henri Michaux's exposure to mescalinic experiments, within the writing of what Valdinoci calls the visceral Universe-Book[148].

By renewing the approach of Language and of Thought, by positing a law of *stereonomy* inside communication that recognizes the potency of the *watermark* (as an invisible inscription within the linguistic indication)[149] – a law that actualizes the visceral-pathemes' impregnation inside Language –, Valdinoci intersects both with René Daumal poetics theorization of the Hindu *Rasa* (रस)[150] and with the Artaldian exploration of breath and embodied rhythms as a process of inviscering cruelty into poetry[151].

[148] See Serge Valdinoci, « Le réel comme livre [the real as book] », *La Science première* (Paris : L'Harmattan, 1997), pp. 135-215.
[149] Serge Valdinoci, *Abrégé d'europanalyse. La pensée analytique et continentale, op. cit.*, p. 19.
[150] René Daumal, *The Powers of the Word (1927-1943)*, trans. M. Polizzotti (San Francisco : City Lights, 1991) and *Rasa or Knowledge of the Self : Essays On Indian Æsthetics and Selected Sanskrit Studies*, trans. L. Landes Levi (New York : New Directions, 1982).
[151] Antonin Artaud, *The Theatre and Its Double*, trans. Mary Caroline Richards (New York : Grove Weidenfeld, 1958) and *Watchfiends & Rack Screams*,

This trend is not only an oldschool fad, but on the contrary it has increased all along the XXth century and has reached to be a concern of major authors, especially in the frame of intense exchanges with American poetry since the Beat Generation, notably **Allen Ginsberg** (1926-1997)[152].

trans. Clayton Echelman (Boston: Exact Change, 1995). Surprisingly, the most important piece of the text « Interjections » is missing in this edition, though formerly translated by C. Echelman (and A. J. Arnold) in *BOMB* No. 7 (New York : New Art Publications, 1983), pp. 42-44.

[152] See Jean-Pierre Bobillot, *Bernard Heidsieck : Poésie action* (Paris : Jean-Michel Place, 1997) & Serge Pey, *Poésie-action* (Paris : Castor Astral, 2018) ; also Philip Auslander « The Performativity of Performance Documentation », *PAJ : A Journal of Performance and Art* (2006) vol. 28, Issue 3 (84), pp. 1–10.

One of the figureheads of this embodied poetics is obviously **Gherasim Luca** (1913-1994), to whom Deleuze is so much indebted as a precursor for *Anti-Œdepus*,[153]. Luca furthered both the work on breathing and uttering, the public-performing body of poetry and the call for an in-corporation of language inside carnal experience.

Who has listened to the imperious and vehement, hammered, phenomenology of self-elucidation into which Gherasim Luca engages himself in « The Other Mister Smith »[154] knows how much Luca leads us,

---

[153] Luca was also acclaimed by Deleuze, though in a quite simplistic manner, for his stuttering work on langage ; see Gilles Deleuze, « He stuttered, » in *Essays Critical and Clinical*, trans. D. W. Smith & M. A. Greco (1993 ; London : Verso, 1998), pp. 107-114.

[154] « L'Autre Mister Smith, » in *Gherasim Luca par Gherasim Luca*, N. & T. Garrel, eds., CD audio (Paris : J. Corti & Héros-Limite, 2001).

by the repeated, stopped, stubborn pulsation of syntagmata, in a relationship of syncopated desires, in a convulsive appetite for sense, which plunges the listener into a state of body (tension, vigilance, greed, alert…) that is the literary impact itself on our physiology (arrested by the breath, by the scansion, by the rhythmic of his cavernous voice of angst, which digs into our carnal state, towards a relational trance in which the imprint of Luca's existence is mingled with our psyche).

And precisely it is not an only linguistic relationship.

What is perceivable here, in the significant variations of our carnal receptivity, in the atmosphere of understanding that reigns and binds to his voice our moment of identity with the World when listening, is that the interpersonal exchange, the sharing of meaning, the intersubjective participation in the intelligence of the world – as a praxis of inter-shaping the psyches – is pre-verbally, prenoeticly or antepredictively felt – below the lexical materia, and on another side of our cognition where descriptions with concepts inherited from twentieth-century linguistics fail[155].

---

[155] *Comment s'en sortir sans sortir*, the film realized in 1989 by Raoul Sangla (Paris: José Corti, 2008) adds, to the sensual modulation of his voice, the postural brilliance of his silhouette and the coiled, sequenced, gesture of his reading with a caught up body.

Luca's famous « Quart d'heure de culture métaphysique [one quarter-hour of metaphysical culture] » In *Le Chant de la carpe* (Paris : José Corti, 1986) engages motor skills in experiences of metaphysical abstractions and ideas *(Time, Death, Emptiness…*), but we can make the same blatant observation in others of his books, even older ones : all the lexicon, all the thematic content, all the rhetoric of Gherasim Luca work massively from perception, from intense and extreme embodied sensations, of which reinvention constitutes the stake itself, thematized inside the text, of the approach of reality that he invites his reader to penetrate with him :

Thus, how could we read « Prendre corps [taking shape] » in *Paralipomènes*[156] without embracing the perceptual anatomy of the erotic relational network that is depicted ; without understanding it as the repercussion of an act of material emergence of senses from this organic experience that supports the lexicon of our understanding of the World ? Because, for Luca, it is precisely about diving, through an intense carnal and sensory work, into the

---

[156] Paris : José Corti, 1986. Luca's « Prendre corps » as been translated in 1999 as « Embody » by M. Tweed and R. Dedourge, accessed January 15, 2018 : https://web.archive.org/web/20070222105400/http://www.info-france-usa.org:80/culture/books/texts/lucas-para.html.

focus of intersubjective relation, and thematizing its reinvention through perceptual stupor, postural electrocution and sensitive dramaturgy. « *I am compelled to invent / a new way to move / to breathe / to exist* » he says, in *The Inventor of Love & Other Works*[157].

Closer to us, **Denis Roche** (1937-2015), although he was, as was already said above, the leading author of the 70's French Textualist scene, insisted on how his writings, deeply related to eroticism and to the scansion of instincts, found in body reactions the immediate verification of the potency of their

---

[157] Trans. L. & J. Semilian (1945 ; Black Widow Press, 2009). See Narciso Aksayam, *Apprendre à prendre corps* (FR-Plancy-L'Abbaye : INgens, 2020).

enticing, being in such a way the great perpetuator of Georges Bataille by actualizing inside poetry an unheralded and outrageous sense of sacrifice, and an undividable interlacing of the most immediate eroticism with the relentless coming of death at every instant[158].

And at last, in the extreme contemporary of Poetry, we cannot omit to name **Christophe Tarkos** (1963-2004), prematurely reaped by malady, who used to perform on stage an amazing art of improvised readings

[158] Within a vast span of writing, Denis Roche, French translator of William Blake, Charles Olson and Ezra Pound, not only insisted with an over-indulgent pen on how intercourse has to hem the fate of our death, like a dreadful dance in front of the Nada (This, he extensively developed in *Éros Éner-gumène* [Obstreperous Eros] (Paris : Le Seuil, 1968) and *Louve basse* [nether she-wolf] (Paris : Le Seuil, 1976)). But Denis Roche's art of photography is also deeply imbued with this concern over the vulnerability of each instant and the timing of desire as a looming form erupting against despair. See Denis Roche, *La Disparition des lucioles* [The disappearance of Fireflies] (Paris : Éditions de l'Étoile, 1982), *Conversations avec le temps* [Conver-sations with time] (Paris : Le Castor astral, 1985) and Gilles Mora, *Denis Roche. Les Preuves du temps* [the proofs/prints of time] (Paris : Seuil/Maison Européenne de la Photo-graphie, 2001).

which deeply involved the embodied materiality of his word[159]. Tarkos both produced a theory of language from immanence and from the sense of immediate identity :

> « There are no words. Words mean nothing. Words have no meaning. There are no words because there is a meaning, meaning has emptied words of all signification, has emptied them completely, nothing remains to the words they're empty emptied sacks that have been emptied, meaning has taken all meaning, left nothing for words, empty shells, meaning debates by itself, doesn't need words, meaning wants everything, has its go, is related to nothing, words are related to nothing »[160]

[159] See Christophe Tarkos, *Ma Langue est Poétique — Selected Work*, trans. S. Doris & C. Wiener, eds. (New York : Roof Books, 2000) or Nina Parish & Emma Wagstaff, eds, *Writing the Real : A Bilingual Anthology of Contemporary French Poetry* (London : Enitharmon Press, 2017) ; and for audio and video records, *L'Enregistré* [The Recorded] (Paris : P.O.L., 2014).
[160] Christophe Tarkos, *Le Signe* = (Paris : P.O.L., 1999)

The first mistake is then to believe that poetry can be defined by words, or by Language. Because it is difficult to discern that words are not real, that they are not isolates, individuations, that they are neither the element of speech nor of the poem, but only one aspect of the raw material, mere secondary cuts, late distinctions, differentiations that have been extracted from a local scale of our human observation, and which we toil to articulate. But also because it is not yet guaranteed within any science, either Linguistics, Biology or Cybernetics, that one whole can be summed up by adding the activities of its parts, neither that belonging to a whole doesn't surreptitiously give to parts some properties which they do not own when they are isolated from it.

The element of Poetry, the raw material of Poetry, is Signification.

And Signification is a state of the body, a felt disposition – atmosphere, mood, affect, ambiance –, and felt as the possibility of a gesture, of an act, of a Behaviour : like adopting a motor posture inside the forces that constitute our World at the moment, the feeling of disposing a transformation within the schema of our accumulating sensations.

And among these states of the body, yes, there are lingual whisperings ; quivering of breath ; grindings of vocal stretched cords ; constellations of ink on the paper grain, skimmed by light, where topologies of dropped initials architect the outlining of our gaze ; positions of lecterns ; atmospheres of miscellany under an isolated framework ; torpors of bereavement, of glory or of allocation ; April appetites ; signs of addresses and of addressees that don't delude, unless…

The event of the poem is then an essential psychic novelty, a redistribution of the split lines of the World of whose space is the spectrum of somatic shades of tonus, of seeping hormones, of ambling respiratory rhythms and of engaged futuritions.

Yet every state of the body is a relational state, Comprehension being the interlacing of the Intelliging and the contingent variation of our Feeling – the entanglement of digit and perception, of gramme and appearing, which forms the alcove where unceasingly happens the rebirth of our subjectivity – as being an offering to the myriad as such. In that sense, Poetry is an intervention in the Relation, active coloration of Between and Among, uncalculated tuning on the trajectory of an existence melody, whose essential phrase happens to be incidentally reoriented.

But upstream to any Language.

That is because, before any word, we are seized by the poetries of mute railway stations, of landscapes on the verge of falling asleep, of inarticulate beasts' vocalizations ; poetries of the next instant riddling our leaned now with dread, and with inebriation ; poetries of a one second lump in our throat, cutting off with a hiccup the intention of a breath, and which we hardly hear when going by the harbor ; archaic poetries of gravel where we crawl, of juice where we swim, of winds where we wander ; primitive poetries of cell membranes, shivering, flickering with per-meability inside the iridescent mist of the World's chemistry. And whose ascendency, with an irrevocable archæology, precedes the beginning of the first poured babble, the chatter of the first emitted juice, the paced rhythm of the first verbal spore. Words barely compose the molecular formula of it, with active substances fleetingly swallowed at the bitter crack of dawn, composition keys for human locks, unlatching mechanisms of unprecedented souls : formal experiments of improbable impacts, obstinate labour of statement towards a human state, psychotropic find collected when strolling among circumstantiated rustlings ; geometry of adjectives for new equilibria, recipe of sememes to taste, indecent algorithms to be unveiled with a morsel of a heart.

And, like inside the hearth of every relation, Poetry is a game of offering in which there a lot to be guessed, a step of mystery on the spongy softness of mosses where Existing ventures our shy extreme toes…

N A R C I S O   A K S A Y A M

NARCISO AKSAYAM, is a poet, a teacher, a physiotherapist, an editor, a literary critic *&* a philosophy researcher ; he teaches *Epistemology & Anthropology* to medical practitioners. His research explores immanence – more specifically as *pathic* – *&* how to learn it according to the measure of the experience of an embodied hæcceity, *i.e.* a finitude certainly lived (in) One, but (in) heave, (in) throng and (in) Becoming.

Thus, as a translator (Gongora, Sloterdijk, Coltrane, Gallagher…), a mystagogue *& an* heteronaut, he explores the penetrative forms of intersubjectivity, in such a way as to model the paths of metamorphosis, of semantics and of asceticism, like shapes of compa-nionship, of support, and of antepredi-cative sharing.

I N G E N S

A LOVING BROZHERHOOD, dedicated to human solitudes of soul, which guesses, cuddles, encloses and harvests poetry. That of the undergrowth, that of the gambling dens,
        that of the hospices, that of the convents.
It shapes a meeting circle, a greenhouse where all artisans of the immensity find to appear as much as to hide, an enclosure of adombration where to reduce oneself,
        a sweet burning crucible where to polymerize.
And slowly its catalog lays out before your eyes the tender flayed drawing that grows and builds an open tomorrow, quartered, wide-eyed, enucleated, like the gazes of the universe fully immersed in its own surprise,
        sublime there and giddy of its own immensity.

REVUES WHERE WE BROWSED IT

L'Homme Précaire [Alain Maison-Ali Lham, 2004]
Aubuscule [Ali Lham-Laurent Hélie, 2007-2012]
#Transitor [DVD multimédia, 2012]
CCP [cipM, 2001-2018]
Philo-Fictions [ONPhI, 2009]
DéZopilant [2011- ∞]
Condition zéro [*to be published…*]

BOOKS WHERE WE FOUND IT

Vanesça come [Anonymous, Éd. Clou dans le Fer, 2003]
Rosalie Superstar [Foutre de Dieu, Cynthia3000,
        2007/ L*Improbable, 2020]
Les Entretiens de Trois-Fontaines [S. Valdinoci, Overblog 2009]
Au Porteur [Anonyme, Éd. INgens 2014]
Doxologie, viatiques pour un voyage en réal-ité
        [Gérard Kponsou, Immensity Notebooks, 2019]
Apprendre à prendre corps - enseignements de Gherasim Luca
        [N. Aksayam, Éd. INgens, 2020]
La Science Avant-première

[Serge Valdinoci, Immensity Notebooks, 2020]
« Voyage loin & haut » [Marc Mehdi Aït-Ali, Coll. DeZopilant, 2021]
Sartre, la Réduction jusqu'à la lie [N. Aksayam, Immensity
    Notebooks, 2021]
Angles morts [SNG.nataʃa **g**ije, 2021]
Le Myste [Brozher Thunder, *to be published…*]

Immensity moments where we grazed it

Poésie : Reims sort le Grand Jeu [Le Cellier, 2021]
Nocturnes de Poésie Contemporaine [itinérant, 2013-2020]
À Portée de main [Maison St Sixte, 2015]
L'Incertitudes des Ombres//La Ralentie [initiatic hypnoesy, 2012-2019,
    with Corso Samara, CharlesH. Ganashine, M.Y.P Bertier]
Phénoménopathie à la 'BalArtdre' [2017-2020]
Laboratoires Transistor [2012-2014]
Soirée Pilote Aubuscule [Library Jean Falala, 2011]
Soirée Transistor [Villa Douce, 2012]
La *C.R.I.É.E* [Centre Antonin Artaud, 2020]
Festivals *CORPUS* [Paris 2015], *Midi-Minuit* [Nantes 2017], *Ut Pictura*
    Poesis [Paris 2019, Poesie isnotdead]

Immensity, you've done well to hide yourself from us, you have done well to throw over our heads this veil, embroidered with pearls, that we call sky. Oh, if you would show yourself! If only once, human intelligence could understand your terrible name !

Alfred de Musset

www.ingens.eu

Fudging Laruelle's Decision

Dépôt légal : 2ème trimestre 2023
EAN : 9782492346064

INGENS
www.ingens.eu

www.ingramcontent.com/pod-product-compliance
Lightning Source LLC
La Vergne TN
LVHW042107190726
843493LV00006B/1392